The Networking Playbook

The Networking Playbook

Transform Your Social Capital into Professional Career Success

Darryl L. Howes, MSc

BEP

BUSINESS EXPERT PRESS

Leader in applied, concise business books

The Networking Playbook:
Transform Your Social Capital into Professional Career Success

Copyright © Business Expert Press, LLC, 2022.

Cover design by Charlene Kronstedt

Back cover photography copyright © www.richardbudd.co.uk, 2021

Interior design by Exeter Premedia Services Private Ltd., Chennai, India

First published in 2022 by
Business Expert Press, LLC
222 East 46th Street, New York, NY 10017
www.businessexpertpress.com

ISBN-13: 978-1-63742-189-5 (paperback)
ISBN-13: 978-1-63742-190-1 (e-book)

Business Expert Press Business Career Development Collection

First edition: 2022

10 9 8 7 6 5 4 3 2 1

For Kev.
And for George and Carl. Two best friends who were brought
back together by happenstance. And connected again.
With grateful thanks for the loving kindness of my immediate
family: Debbie, Nicki, Steph, Amanda, and Karl.

—London, January 2021

Description

Is your career headed where it needs to go? Disappointed and disengaged by job interviews? Don't sit back and wait for things to happen. Get more done! Design your career and deliver your life!

People networking must be an essential element of any professional and personal development program. Your individual success proceeds from building valuable relationships that advance your life project and supercharge the achievement of your goals.

Management of your networking activity isn't about deceit or Machiavellian sharp practice. Instead, it involves starting with the end in mind, thinking about your direction of travel and having a values-based route map to get there.

Networking is not a nil sum game—you win/I lose. Instead, it's about making the pie bigger in terms of opportunities. Let's work together, find out what we have in common, harness our creativity and make the pie as big as possible! Turn up! Follow up! And keep it up!

Whether you are a first-time or experienced networker, *The Networking Playbook* will coach you in the skills required for success, allowing you to plan and control your future. Introducing valuable insights and information from psychology, sociology, and anthropology, it's the one career advice book that puts you in charge of successful networking.

Keywords

career; professional; networking; job search; career advice; personal development; networking playbook; success; management; coach; plan

Contents

Testimonials xi

Preface xiii

Acknowledgments.. xv

Introduction xvii

Chapter 1   What Is a Playbook? (The Playbook Play)......................1

Chapter 2   Strategic Business Networking....................................11

Chapter 3   But I'm Not a Networker … (The Imposter Play).........17

Chapter 4   Networking as a Process (The Process Play) 29

Chapter 5   Getting the Message Across (The Bongs Play)..............43

Chapter 6   How to Craft Our Key Messages (The Who,
              Why, and What Play) 51

Chapter 7   Moving Around a Room (The Dunbar's
              Number Play)..61

Chapter 8   Building Mentor and Advocate Networks
              (The Mentor Play) 67

Chapter 9   Social Media and Networking (The Know Your
              Audience Play) 81

Chapter 10   What Happens Next? (The NEXTworking Play) 97

Chapter 11   When Our Networking Is NOT Working
              (The Troubleshooting Play)..105

Chapter 12   A Final Word … (Are We Agile or Fragile?—the
              Final Play) 113

References and Further Reading..115

About the Author...123

Index 125

Testimonials

"Darryl is one of the best networkers in the UK. If you need to understand the who, what, when, where, and how of people networking, get in touch with him."—**Derek Arden, International Negotiation Expert, and author of Win Win: How to Get a Winning Result from Persuasive Negotiations, London, England**

"The book goes into much greater detail than any other book on networking I have read; yet allows a person some latitude as to how they will network, via the author's 'scaffolding' approach. Although extensively researched and abundant with technical references for those who wish to have them, the book is extremely readable. The summary bullet points at the end of each chapter were invaluable in helping me plot my networking roadmap and routes. This is a wonderful book ... really something special."—**Tim Durkin, Leadership Expert, Certified Speaking Professional, and author of Moving from Promise to Performance: 17 Sure-Fire Strategies for Better Results at Work and at Home, Dallas TX**

"Darryl Howes has written the opposite of a text book on networking. It's a playbook that's action orientated, dispels the most common myths around networking such as 'just be yourself' or 'find your tribe' and provides not only relevant examples but signposts the reader to deepen their practice and mastery of such a vital topic. A book that can not only help you develop your social capital but also your life. Highly recommended!"—**Steven D'Souza, Senior Client Partner, Korn Ferry. Author of 'Brilliant Networking' and Co-Author of the award winning 'Not Knowing' trilogy http://www.stevendsouza.com, London, England**

"This is a well written book which will be useful to those starting out in their careers who wish to learn more about the art and importance of networking and to those with more experience, but who wish to improve their effectiveness. Far from being a 'dry' textbook, it is written in an engaging and easily understandable style which makes it a very enjoyable read."—**John M. Hodson, Senior Vice President, Handelsbanken, London, England**

"*This book will be enormously valuable to anyone who needs to improve their networking skills—in other words, almost all of us. It is packed with practical advice and insights into how to build up effective relationships which will help us get where we want to go not only in business but in life, supported all the way through by compelling evidence and lively anecdotes. What comes through strongly is how none of these efforts will succeed unless we are sincere and authentic in the way we reach out to others.*"—**Charles Fowler, Chair, Human Values Foundation, London, England**

"*Darryl is an inspiration when it comes to networking. He has encouraged me to expand my horizons and gain the confidence to reach out to others. On publication day, I was first in the queue at my local bookstore.*"—**Stuart M. Leeds, I/O Psychology Master of Science student, Bath, England**

"*This extremely well-researched book will be invaluable to all who wish to implement or develop their personal networking strategies. During my extensive business career, I have consistently stressed the importance of networking to my management team. Some got it, many did not. This book will be invaluable to those who may know what they should be doing, but none the less struggle to implement it. The author guides and advises on all aspects of effective networking and the Strategic Business Networking© framework really hits home, allowing you to 'get it' quicker and better than any other networking book I have read.*"—**Godfrey Lancashire, Business Adviser, Mentor and Coach. Cofounder and co-owner, London House International, Dorset, England**

Preface

We are about to witness a seismic shift in the world of work. And I don't mean all this stuff about working from home, or teleworking, or flexible working, or whatever today's buzzword is. That has been going on to a greater or lesser extent since the word "telecommuting" was formally coined in the early 1970s.

No, it's something deeper than that. We are going to witness the acceleration of a model that challenges long-held beliefs around what it means to be a manager or to be an employee. What "work" means in common parlance will also change.

I'm not saying this will happen overnight and, as William Gibson (as cited in Pettman, 2009) said, "The future is already here—it's just not evenly distributed," but change is coming and, like a wildfire, if it catches it is likely to be rapid.

Rather, I mean that the processes initiated by large-scale freelancing platforms such as Upwork, People per Hour, and so on will develop further. Of course, books have talked about this before. "The Start Up of You," by LinkedIn's key founder, Reid Hoffman, is one particularly good example.

But this time, it won't be some form of lifestyle choice, with the option to return to a "secure" job if it doesn't suit you.

No. Largescale depletion of traditional workforces will require people to become freelancers out of necessity and to stay that way. And as traders of time for money, we will quickly need to get to grips with these models. Or instead find that we have little or no means of income at all.

I don't say this to scare you. Every challenge can be met, but it's sometimes useful to have some help along the way.

This book will not school you in disciplines such as marketing, start-up finance, or prospecting for customers, although you would do well to learn these things if solo-preneurship beckons. It will tackle something much more fundamental and, in a strange way, easier for us all. If we behave as human beings.

I'm talking about the power of people networks to help us achieve what we want.

The ability to build, manage, and leverage networks is going to be highly important, if not essential, to survive and thrive in shiny new versions of our respective economies. Again, there's nothing new about this and many people have been happily cultivating networks for many years and profiting from them. I'm one of them. And if I can do it, so can you.

The point is, whether we are totally new to networking or just a little bit rusty through not having practiced it for a while, we are all going to have to get a little better and bigger at it.

As the saying goes, "Go Big, or Go Home."

Acknowledgments

The Gratitude Attitude (The Gratitude Play)

Thoughts, ideas, and actions rarely arise in a vacuum. There are many people who I am grateful to for allowing me to benefit from their experience and professionalism. They have shown me, taught me, counseled me, and guided me, often in the subtlest of ways. All have informed the writing of this book. I blame an imperfect memory and offer my apologies to anyone I have missed:

Adrian Swinscoe

Peter B. Roach

Chris Sandford

Graham Scillitoe

Tony Sexton

Derek Arden

Andy Lopata

Heather Townsend

Adam Grant

John Lees

Jackie Jenks OBE

Duncan J Watts

Bryan Treherne MBE

Reid Hoffman

Claire Galmiche

Charles Fowler

David Gurteen

Lynne J. Millward

Adrian Banks

Almuth McDowall

Mavis Cracknell

Susan Luke Evans

George Howes

Carl Smith

William O'Sullivan

Nicolette Ladoulis

Bart Sangster

Ingrid Covington

Duncan Watts

Caroline Goyder

Kim Stephenson

Martine Robins

Peter Saville

Frances Brown

Richard Wiseman

Albert-László Barabási

Herminia Ibarra

David Seaton

Shirley Seaton

Brené Brown

Katrina Ramage

Mark Granovetter

Stew Friedman

Anna McAfee

Special thanks to the team at Business Expert Press: Scott, Charlene, Melissa, Sheri, Sung and, of course, Vilma for all your help and support.

Introduction

We all have it within us to be better networkers. And in being so, better managers of our careers.

Work is important to society and to individuals. Ask anyone who is unfulfilled in their job, or unable to work, about the effect on their identity and personal self-worth and we'll not be surprised by the answer.

The management point is also important. We can occasionally feel helpless in the context of our careers. Just corks bobbing along on the tide of economics, commerce, or any other external event we choose to name, making it difficult for us to see beyond the present.

But it is also within us to resist this.

Stephen Covey*, the author of "The 7 Habits of Highly Effective People," wrote that we have a choice: "to act and not feel acted upon."

This book is dedicated to providing a plan, with actionable steps to promote good career management and, by definition, good networking practice.

Perhaps we're an early-stage professional looking to take that all-important first step up the career ladder. Or maybe we are considering changing career and need to look at how we can complete the transition and reinvent ourselves. Or simply at a career crossroads, feeling stuck and not quite knowing which direction to take.

My hope is that this book will help to develop strategies to make the most of our networks, our careers, and ultimately our lives. In doing so, we'll enjoy greater personal happiness and fulfillment.

And, hopefully, the end of the global pandemic of 2020/2021 will provide us all with an opportunity to reconnect with loved ones, kith and kin, business partners, work colleagues, employers, mentors and mentees, and so on.

There's a great song by The Waterboys, the British-Irish folk rock band formed in Edinburgh in 1983. It was written and produced by a very talented and perceptive man, Mike Scott.

Do listen closely to the words the next time you hear it. Like Mike, I'd like to try and help you see "The Whole of the Moon."

—Darryl L. Howes, MSc

January 2021

*For those who do not know the name, there is a brilliant analysis of the impact of Professor Covey's work within the *Harvard Business Review* article, "Stephen R. Covey Taught Me Not to Be Like Him" by Greg McKeown.

CHAPTER 1

What Is a Playbook? (The Playbook Play)

"The Coach"

Definition: Playbook / pleɪbʊk/ {noun}—North American, meaning "a book containing a sports team's strategies and plays, especially in American football." A networking playbook contains all the pieces and parts that make up your go-to approach for getting things done and achieving your networking objectives. It includes your own personal "process workflows, standard operating procedures and cultural values that shape a consistent response—the play."

Image © 2021 Daniel Byron

I have been thinking about writing a book for the last five years. It's probably partly the age thing and the thoughts one has as time ticks by on a life.

Another motivation is to try to play a very small part in leveling up society. I believe that opportunity should be available to the brightest and best, whatever their background or ethnicity. Networking is a huge part of social advancement. I'm no social commentator, but there's a lot that could be done to combat the many forms of unwarranted privilege that exist in our societies.

I also think I have something to offer. Not through blind bravado, but because I have been there and done it (or my version of whatever "it" is).

This is a book about people networking. But unlike some others, it will be a combination of what to do and, crucially, the why.

The why will cover why the book's suggestions (the "plays") actually work in practice. What effect will they have on the reader and others? What basis do they have in verified research around the social sciences? The book's subject matter will draw upon psychology, sociology, and anthropology—but will match this against in-the-field commercial experience, debunking myths as it goes along.

The why will also provide interesting and insightful answers and provide a route map for individuals to decide on their own networking strategies.

I can't direct people on exactly what to do. They generally do as they please. But I can teach basic principles allowing them to work out and then employ their own Playbook. This is an important lesson around both motivation and memory—we learn and internalize better when something has semantic value; that is, when it is unique to ourselves in its meaning.

As a post-COVID world seeks to reconnect at a face-to-face level, this will be a useful book with wide appeal.

I also want to say a little about "Values."

People often ask me, "How can I prepare to become a (better) networker?"

This is both simple and complex, because my answer generally involves a suggestion that the person try to think about their personal values.

Now values are funny things. Some we seem to inherit from our caregivers, others just grow within us based on experience. Most people articulate them as "What I believe in" or "The way I live" or "What I consider to be important."

One of my mentors, Charles Fowler, Chair of the Human Values Foundation based in the United Kingdom, makes a very good point. People can often quite easily say what they think their values are. But they can have extreme difficulty in acting upon them, or "living" them consistently.

This isn't a criticism of people. Something we all have to grapple with, having first become clear on what our values are, is how we put them into action.

And this rises above what might be called superficial thinking around eating well, exercising, getting enough sleep, and so on. These things are comparatively easy when it comes to addressing the really difficult things that the messiness of life throws at us: bereavement, divorce, or even dealing with teenage offspring!

So, if you and I want to get better at people networking, we could do a whole lot worse than to consider our values. Why? Because they will serve as a litmus test for how we behave toward people and how they behave toward us.

And networking life gets a whole lot easier, if we can talk about our values clearly and concisely and then find others who share them.

So, I've said it. That's my best advice for you right here, right now: Think and act values.

I also want to give an early callout to gender. For too long, male activity alone has been the focus of so-called "real" networking, whether that be at the golf club, frat house, or masonic lodge. Recent years have thankfully seen this view change and society has witnessed a proliferation of female networking groups—some women only, some mixed gender.

To be clear, although there appear to be some differences in the way that women and men network (see, e.g., Yang et al. 2019), there is no definitive research, which infers that one gender is better than the other. So, if you are a woman reading this, all the suggested tools and techniques in this book apply to you in exactly the same way as they would anyone else.

I'd go further in expressing a personal view that, in my experience, women can make better networkers than men. I've reached this conclusion over many years, and my ideas rest on the tendency of most women to listen better when in a networking context and act in a more collegiate, noncompetitive, and generous way.

For me, women have no problem in playing the long game when networking and are more likely to focus on personal aspects of a relationship in the first instance and build the commercial aspects from there.

So there, please do carry on reading whoever you are!

I have used "I" language in some of the previous paragraphs. I'm sorry. We will now use "we" language from now on. This is a good point to clarify, because it's a networking journey that we embark on together.

What's Important (The Importance Play/the Importance *of* Play)

Career Management ...

The job market has changed. A combination of technology and rapid organizational development has jettisoned the past and made predicting future trends almost impossible. Many experts now even question the concept of a career.

Some articulate the recruitment shift as one from push to pull. Rather than a job-seeker applying for a role in the traditional way, companies are on the lookout for talent and are adept at making the first approach. And social media is one of the key tools for this.

In addition, traditional talent management programs incur high recruitment costs. The uncertainties of some assessment and selection processes mean that a large proportion of vacancies arise through the unadvertised job market.

These roles are never actively promoted. They tend to come about through immediate need for a talent solution and the knowledge that someone knows someone else who is a good fit for the vacancy.

Hence these opportunities are accessed via who we know (and who knows us, and what we do). This trend partly explains the growth of employee referral schemes, where existing employees are encouraged to introduce new people to the business.

It's the same for the growing army of self-employed, who need to look after their own career management as much as anyone, whether a contractor, freelancer, or solo-preneur.

Career rewards are good for the top people, but it's a VERY competitive market. Never has it been more important to find a way to stand out from the crowd. In the words of career specialist, John Lees, (and if self-promotion sounds unpleasant to you), it's about self-projection.

Networking ...

Self-projection involves getting ourselves out there. We can't network from the shed in the yard!

As humans, we are essentially social animals. Our development across time has hinged principally upon our ability to live and function in the company of others.

Of course, there are many shades to this. But just as there are many different types of people and personality, there are many different forms of networking and networker. Yes, there are a few people who are born networkers—but many more who recognize networking for what it is; a learnable skill that can develop and improve over time.

The Theme That Links the Two ...

Success takes teamwork. No one can do it on their own. All successful people rely on a network of mentors, advisers, and confidantes.

Nurturing key relationships that can facilitate career and personal development is what all successful people do. And they build and refer to this network continually and consistently.

Interacting with new people is important. We never know who we might meet and the effect they may have on our professional life and career.

When it comes to building a relationship with a former POTUS, Richard Branson's Necker Island property isn't just a holiday retreat ...

Should We Play at Networking?

The title to this section mentions "play?"

Yes, that's because we should try to have fun when we network. Otherwise, what's the point? And we are not talking play *at* it, we are talking play *with* it.

It may not feel much like play at first. For some, it may feel more like torture!

But every networking guru under the sun confirms that, after a bit of practice, we'll all warm to it.

Don't treat it like a game. That implies competition.

Treat it like life. And learn to love it!

Are we about to experience a "New-Age of Enlightenment?"

Hi there.

I'm your guide and mentor to help you navigate this book.

This section is the first of what I'm calling an Information Box. You'll spot them here and there throughout the book.

They are intended to be of interest if you'd like to read further into a topic or find out more. They are also designed to help you think. And, as with most things including people networking, thinking is good.

Sometimes the heading at the top of the box will provide a clue to the content. Sometimes it won't. Sometimes it will just sound weird!

At the time of writing, the COVID pandemic is still waging its war across the globe. Some lucky people in the Western world can see light at the end of the tunnel. Others cannot and will not for some time. News reports in my own country talk of the virus being around for some time yet to come—a "new normal" as some like to call it.

The effect of the pandemic has been wide and terrible. Lives lost, relationships ruined, children orphaned. I could add further to this troubling list.

But dare I suggest that perhaps there have been some positive effects?

Speaking personally, my wife and I have both been working from home over the last 12 months. Having had "corporate" careers, we both now act as consultants.

I have suddenly realized, after nearly 40 years of marriage (mostly happy, I'm pleased to say), what a fantastically warm and welcoming telephone voice she has. And she seems to be so much more efficient and organized than I have hitherto (and quite wrongly) given her credit.

She hasn't said yet what she notices about me!

To take another view, how many children have gained valuable insight into the working lives of their parents? How many teenagers have been energized, or dissuaded, by seeing at firsthand what their parents do for a living? Have future careers been hinted at during this time?

Finally, am I the only one who has found their energy and motivation greater, their creativity boosted and their critical thinking just a little bit sharper?

And this leads me on to the main point (I get there in the end!):

Are we about to experience a "New-Age of Enlightenment?"

Author's note: What exactly was "The Age of Enlightenment?"

OK, not for the first time, we are going to take a short journey into the academic mind. Academics love to argue—or at least the ones I know do!

I heard once of a person who sat on a committee consisting of two academics, two professional practitioners, and them. Discussions often resembled a boxing match. They were the ones who had to break up the fights and sound the ringside bell at the end of each argument!

I digress.

Scholars disagree on pretty much everything relating to what has been called the Age of Enlightenment; when it started, what period it covered, who was involved, what was discussed, and even which of many countries could have been the instigator.

I'm referring of course to a period in history around the 18th/19th centuries, which spawned intellectual movements committed to science and, above all else, individual critical thinking, separate from the doctrines and dogmas of Church, State, or Monarchy.

Across the globe, leading exponents were Rene Descartes, Immanuel Kant, Voltaire, Thomas Jefferson, and Benjamin Franklin. In my own country, the United Kingdom, the philosophers Francis Bacon, John Locke, and Thomas Paine (or plain "Tom Paine" in the less formal United States) are all cited.

Others can be said to have laid down groundwork as early instigators of Britain's Industrial Revolution; and, of course, this baton was carried further by those who developed and profited from the many technological advancements that came from the new ways of thinking.

Again, in the United Kingdom, the famed Lunar Society of 1775 was so called because the relatively small network of only 14 core members met during the time of a full moon. The extra light provided by this moon-phase made the journey home easier and safer in the absence of modern street lighting.

Its members included free-thinking scientists and industrialists such as William Small, James Watt, Joseph Priestley, Josiah Wedgwood, and Erasmus Darwin (an early abolitionist for the dreadful and dehumanizing slave trade, and grandfather of Charles Darwin).

It's perhaps little known that the wider tentacles of the group (all networks have strong or weak ties, as we shall see later) spread out to Thomas Jefferson, a pupil of Thomas Small. At the time, Small was professor of Natural Philosophy at the College of William and Mary in Williamsburg, Virginia.

And, as every good American knows, Thomas Jefferson collaborated closely with Benjamin Franklin in the drafting of the Declaration of Independence.

And, furthermore, Franklin, himself an early global politician and master networker, went on to create his own version of the Lunar Society, which he called the "Junto." Franklin described this collective as "like-minded aspiring artisans and tradesmen who hoped to improve themselves while they improved their community."

There's nothing new under the sun in networking!

So where am I going with this self-evident network of Key Influencers of the day?

Well, close to where I have visited many times while working with the London Institute of Banking and Finance, lies the 202-feet-tall

Monument to the Great Fire of London, codesigned by the famed British architect, Sir Christopher Wren.

By design, the structure also stands 202 feet from the site of a bakery in Pudding Lane. This was where, in 1666, all the action is said to have started.

A strange and compelling fact is that the Monument is not just a memorial column. It was also intended to be a large-scale scientific instrument (a bit like the CERN Large Hadron Collider of its day!). The 311 steps up to the top, each 6 inches tall, were incorporated by the other originator, Robert Hooke, to facilitate measurement of changes in atmospheric pressure.

The Great Fire seems to have been instrumental in ridding London of another global pandemic: The Great Plague. It is said to have aided the killing off of the black rats and their accompanying fleas that carried the plague virus.

So perhaps the end of that pandemic was the herald of something new and exciting in those times?

The late historian Roy Porter, a former Director of the Wellcome Institute for the History of Medicine at University College London, had an informed and highly pertinent view that "The Enlightenment was British first, and that the modern world started here" in these islands.

So I ask again, following another dreadful pandemic, are we now ready for a more expansive, free-thinking, individualized view of our world? Are we about to experience a "New-Age of Enlightenment?" And will we be more connected and networked as a result?

Take Action

- Make your playbook your go-to approach for getting your networking done.
- Take responsibility.
- Play at it. And learn to love it!

CHAPTER 2

Strategic Business Networking©

Strategic Business Networking recognizes there are different strokes for different folks. It won't seek to impose a rigid system on the individual. Rather, it provides a framework or scaffold upon which the individual's personal and authentic way of doing things can hang.

Strategic Business Networking—let's break that down.

The **Strategic** element acknowledges there needs to be a plan, coupled with some forethought around what we want to achieve (*"start with the end in mind,"* another of Professor Covey's 7 Habits).

Business means that we are operating in a commercial context. And if we think that finding a job or advancing our career isn't necessarily "business," then we perhaps need to think again.

Organizations of any kind need people to perform. This is easy to understand if we work for Microsoft, a business operating in a sector which is "privately" owned and profit motivated.

But it is also true of the public sector (local, regional, or national government) where ratepayers and voters need elected officials or unelected employees to come up with creative solutions, often against a backdrop of ever-reducing central budgets.

And so also of the often unfairly characterized "third sector," the haunt of *"unreconstructed class war heroes, sandal wearing entrepreneurs, communitarian do-gooders with myopic spheres of interest, bicycles and brown rice."* Here, to do more with less (doing more good with a smaller pot of funding) also requires a businesslike approach.

Never mix business and pleasure the adage goes, but certainly, the two are not exclusive; the growth of corporate hospitality is a testament to this. But "business" does draw a distinction between a professional conversation around career, work, or commercial development that may have a specific aim and, conversely, an informal social chat with friends at the bar.

And Strategic Business Networking has another twist. It emphasizes the importance of follow up. Google the word "networking" and it will return hundreds of thousands (millions?) of hits that talk about behavior at networking events. What to say, what to do, where to go.

But networking doesn't end when the venue catering staff clear the plates and glasses. In fact, all experienced networkers realize this is only the beginning of good networking practice.

What happens *after* the event is just as important as our behavior during the event, if not more so.

Strategic Business Networking is also built around the three "Ups":

- Turn Up
- Follow Up
- Keep it Up

If applied in the right way, these three things will enhance a very valuable resource that each of us have and own. It's called Social Capital.

According to Hanifan, 1916, the textbook definition of this phrase would go something like

> *those tangible substances (that) count for most in the daily lives of people; namely good will, fellowship, sympathy and social intercourse among the individuals and families that make up a social unit* (as cited in Putnam 2000, 19).

But there's a simpler alternative:

Social Capital is what people say about us when we are not in the room.

Start as we mean to go on (The Self-less Play)

All this talk of strategy, commerce, and competition may have us thinking about self-interest and how to get ahead of others.

But self-projection through networking and career management doesn't mean we must become selfish in our actions.

There's a better, self-less, method …

A Story …

A first-time author was advised to promote her work in the usual way: through a formal book launch.

But she had other idseas.

*Rather than follow the trend, she decided just to invite friends, family, colleagues, and supporters to a party. She didn't want the book to be the focus: instead, **she** wanted to celebrate **them** and the warmth of their mutual friendship.*

At a normal book launch, people are encouraged to gather around the author while she/he signs the books, sometimes adding a personalized message. The buyer then pays and moves on, satisfied with their purchase.

The author flipped this model. She arranged for a single copy of the book to be circulated amongst the group and invited those attending to sign it and, if they wanted, to add a comment.

This copy has pride of place in the author's home.

(I am indebted to Adrian Swinscoe, mentor, CX expert and author of Rare Business, How to Wow and Punk CX for this vignette).

We can view this story as a metaphor for networking practice.

Are we networking just for ourselves or for other people also? Do we want to be the networker who sets up an opportunity solely for personal commercial gain or simple self-promotion?

Or:

Do we want to take a wider view and be the person who celebrates success in the company of others, receives gratitude from others gracefully, and expresses gratitude to those who contributed?

The person who gives and asks for nothing in return …

You can't have your cake and eat it, the old saying goes. Many people take the view that professional life is about having a bigger slice of the cake—often at the expense of others sat at the same table. Economists refer to this as a zero-sum game: We win, they lose.

This book promotes a different approach: make the cake bigger and share the bounty.

This way, everyone stands a chance of benefitting from the goodwill that Strategic Business Networking can deliver.

Optimal Distinctiveness ... or Weak Ties?

Optimal Distinctiveness

As humans, we are motivated to form groups and alliances. The strength of our affiliation with other individuals is dependent in part upon the interests we share.

But also important is the nature of the common interest. The rarer a group value, skill or, experience, the more likely it is to facilitate a bond.

Consider the example of two people who meet and learn they share a passion for mountain climbing. How much stronger the bond when they subsequently discover they have each conquered Mount Everest. And stronger still if both completed the more difficult North Ridge route.

And yet stronger, when they can both claim they attained this high-altitude feat without the aid of oxygen masks.

This somewhat extreme case of "optimal distinctiveness" is what Adam Grant, psychologist and Wharton Business School professor, refers to as "uncommon commonality"—people are said to be happier in groups where this is available.

During a conversation, our networking strategy could include searching for common ground and seeing how this might then develop into optimal distinctiveness.

Weak Ties

But before we jump in to explore shared experiences with our conversational partners, optimal distinctiveness is based upon a principle of equilibrium. This says we want to fit in, but we might also want to stand out. We want to be alike, but different.

Over 40 years ago, a young researcher called Mark Granovetter proposed the concept of "weak ties." Now a professor at Stanford, Granovetter's ideas question the virtue of strong ties, such as those that might form through exclusive networks.

In our example, anyone who has not climbed Mount Everest via the North Ridge and without oxygen would find it difficult to break into this somewhat specialist conversation!

Granovetter makes the claim that a more effective, perhaps more agile, networking strategy is through the employment of weak ties within, across, and beyond these strong and exclusive associations.

The paradox he identifies is that weak ties promote the integration of individuals. They avoid the alienation that some strong-tie associations create.

A more enlightened networking strategy is to have a mix of both strong tie and weak tie networks. In other words, those who we can call upon and instantly share a bond. And those who are more distant by relationship and interests, but nonetheless feel part of our network.

Weak ties also provide valuable outward-looking scope. It's often said that whatever the industry, whatever the situation, the basic challenges of business are similar.

This being the case, access to someone like us, facing similar problems, is valuable. Regardless of whether they are doing so in the context of another country, language, or culture. If we need to solve a problem by thinking outside the box, these types of connections can be very useful.

As Granovetter says, weak ties are "indispensable to individuals' opportunities."

Further Support for Weak Ties?

Robert D. Putnam is well-known for his work on the decline of prosocial behaviors in modern society. These days, are we less inclined to give service to our neighbors, friends, or community?

As a social scientist, Professor Putnam talks of networks that are "exclusive" and those that are "inclusive."

Exclusive networks bind us to close, sometimes elite, gatherings (in the United Kingdom, the public-school neck-tie represents one example). It's impossible, or at least difficult, for nonmembers to break in.

Conversely, inclusive networks act as a bridge across exclusivity and offer the power to connect with others who might otherwise remain outside our networking field of vision.

Putnam's analogy of referring to the two types as "Social Superglue" and "Social WD40" respectively, offers a good shorthand for understanding the effect of exclusive and inclusive networks on social cohesion in an increasingly global village.

Take Action

- Develop your own gratitude attitude.
- Make the cake bigger.
- We want to stand out. But we also want to fit in.
- Turn up. Follow up. Keep it up.

CHAPTER 3

But I'm Not a Networker ... (The Imposter Play)

Networking Myths

It's intriguing to consider the advice that's often given out about networking. Let's ponder some quandaries. Not everything in networking is as it seems.

Myth Number 1—"You've Got to Work the Room"

A Google search of this phrase yields over 84 million results.

Much networking advice around how we should behave tends to lack context. And without context, it becomes meaningless and of limited value to those of us looking for sound, practical direction.

For example, being able to "work the room" surely depends on how big the room is? Carnegie Hall? The two million square feet of the National Exhibition Centre in Birmingham, England? Bus stop queue? (Yes, standing in a queue is an opportunity to network!).

The process of "working a room" might mean different things to different people. Perhaps we've experienced meeting the sales networker who believes they should relieve themselves of as many business cards as possible. It's a "spray and pray" technique: the card is handed to us and they move on—quickly.

What impressions are we left with? Certainly not positive ones.

The argument here is for us to have our own personalized version of "Work the Room," which adjusts according to the circumstances. It also becomes a work in progress where we can reflect and build upon past successes.

As for a more bombastic interpretation of the phrase? Well, it may be better for us to leave that to our favorite Hollywood movie celebrity as they "work the crowd."

Myth Number 2—"It's Easy, Just Be Yourself"

The problem with "being ourselves" is the assumption that we know who "we" are.

We can bring to mind other people for some help with this concept. Younger friends and associates who have a strong sense of who they are. Maybe older work colleagues who, despite their age, are not confident of their core self. Certainly, age is not a predictor of knowing ourselves.

We hear a lot these days about being authentic in everything we do; be ourselves, be real, and people will accept us for who we are.

But who we are might require further investigation. And, by the way, we can try this at home. Like a solo version of "knock down ginger," we can knock on our own door and see who answers!.

Consider for example our roles as sisters or brothers, mothers or fathers, daughters or sons, nephews or uncles. In each of these contexts are we really the same person, or could our behavior be determined by what is expected of us?

In this way, being ourselves implies a degree of flexibility that is more like Shakespeare's "All the world's a stage," where we play "many parts" (take a look at Professors Ben (C). Fletcher and Karen J. Pine's book *Flex: Do Something Different* for more on this theme).

The scientist Peter Senge famously said, "*People don't resist change. They resist being changed.*" We are not asking ourselves to change our core.

Instead of using authenticity as a measure, Adam Grant suggests that sincerity holds the key. In other words, rather than be content with our authentic selves, we should instead push upward toward a higher, ideal version.

Grant's work is influenced by that of Brian Little (more of Brian later). Psychologists talk about personality traits as a means of assessing people. Prof, Little believes that "*There are fates beyond traits.*"

This means that, whatever our personality questionnaires may "reveal" about us, we don't have to be hidebound by either personality traits or personality types. Neither should be viewed as our destiny. And we perhaps ought not to pay too much close attention to those psychometric tests we have taken.

These ideas also chime with the work of Professor Carol Dweck of Stanford University on the topic of fixed and growth mindset.

A fixed mindset holds that talent alone is responsible for success, whereas in a growth mindset people believe their abilities can be developed through dedication and hard work. Intelligence and some talent may also matter, but they are just the start point.

What does this mean for "Just be yourself?" And, in particular, for someone who might feel that networking just isn't right for them?

Well, perhaps it might be better to focus on who or what we want to be and where we want our personal project to take us. If we really need to be a better networker, let's give it a go.

Professor Grant provides an example from his own experience. As an introvert by nature, he targeted an alternative self by leveraging his passion for communication. This allowed him to reframe and overcome his dread of public speaking.

There is nothing wrong in aiming to become an improved version of ourselves. And by starting from the outside in, we can try this persona on and act it out in a sincere way without damaging our credibility or reputation with others.

Myth Number 3—"Find Your Tribe"

This is an interesting one. And perhaps a situation where the modern world has some impact.

Yes, humans are social animals. But the late Sir Ken Dodd, a long-standing and respected UK comedian, told the story of what he considered to be the oldest joke in the world.

Sir Ken said it's about how the people in *this* village think that the villagers *next door, over the hillside*, are a funny old lot. If we like, it's a version of the English making fun of Scottish parsimony, those from the deep south of America joshing about "Yankees," and all of us telling jokes about the good people of Ireland (including the Irish themselves—they are master joke-tellers!).

Much of the science around this comes from research about "in groups" and "out groups." In other words, how easy it is for us to form affiliations with some fellow humans but, just as easily, how we can emphasize our differences with other groups.

And, of course, feelings of difference can lead to antagonism and more. Politicians know this very well.

But so much that is good about the modern world is about new opportunities to connect with people. And, remembering those "weak tie" connections, in ways not previously thought possible.

And, rather than emphasize differences through the formation of exclusive groups (possibly even hard-to-join cliques), best networking practice can exist by celebrating diversity through multilayered, multicultural connections.

Once again, we never quite know who we might meet and the effect they may have on our lives and careers.

Find your tribe has a place. But it's not the only place.

Types and Traits

There is a degree of philosophical argument about what is meant by types and traits. Indeed, psychologists love to argue over the meaning of words even before they decide on how the words might be used!

But then again, as a very eminent academic psychologist once said to me, *"Darryl you do know that most psychologists are mad, don't you?"*

The first thing to say is that this subheading has been very carefully worded. My personal view is that there can be *both* types and traits. It's not a case of either one or the other (if so, I might have said types *or* traits. Language matters!).

An example of a "type" psychological theory would be that proposed by Professor Hans Eysenck. In the extreme of type theory, people are placed in definite boxes to describe their personality and therefore ways of behaving. In fact, to complicate matters further, Eysenck called them "dimensions" not types.

So far so good?

Some psychological theories can be a little bit like "old wine in new bottles," meaning they are the extension of earlier thinking. There's nothing wrong with this. It's one of the ways that science advances. Type (or dimensions) can be traced right back to the second-century AD Roman physician, Galen, who talked about categorizing people in terms of four "Humors"—melancholic, choleric, phlegmatic, and sanguine.

Turning to trait theory as proposed by say, Raymond Cattell, personality and behavior is explained more as being somewhere along a continuum (you are on a train journey: Are you boarding the train, at the end of the journey about to disembark, or at one of the stations in-between?).

But all this starts to get confusing when we acknowledge that Cattell talked about source traits and surface traits and the extent to which his assessment of these factors overlapped. From one point of view, source traits can sound a little like types. And Cattell called them fundamental dimensions!

So where does this leave us in this little enigma of a psychological maze?

Well, I'm going to argue that there may not be a huge difference between types and traits. With apologies for the ripe language, they could well be "two cheeks from the same butt!"

But I say this quietly because mad psychologists with shotguns can be very dangerous beasts indeed ...

So, What's to Be Done?

Sometimes, it can be easy to talk ourselves down. Psychologists refer to these internal dialogues as limiting self-beliefs.

So, let's say we hold the view that we can't network, that we're "no good" with people because we are of an introverted nature, or we just don't feel like doing it.

Fortunately, a lot more has been written in recent times about how we can be more flexible in our thoughts, feelings, and behaviors (again, Professors Ben C. Fletcher and Karen J. Pine's book *Flex: Do Something Different* is an excellent example).

Quite often we'll need to "Fake It Until We Make It." All we're doing here is suggesting to ourselves that we'll need to play a part-time temporary role. In this example, as a competent, confident networker.

We can then decide to step outside our normal, default character with the promise that we don't have to stay indefinitely and can return to the default when we're ready.

But let's not forget that for many of us, we're talking here about behavior change and a big one at that.

In the corporate world, it's said that up to 80 percent of change programs fail. Why? Because organizations often try to do too much too quickly.

True behavior change that really lasts comes about through taking and repeating small steps. It's a process of gradual, slow build.

It's the same with networking. We shouldn't try to do too much too soon. We should work toward measurable and realistic milestones.

For example, we could say to ourselves "At this business breakfast, I'm going to initiate conversation with three people I haven't met before." There are some suggested milestones and more about target setting in the following section..

Once the target is achieved, we can relax and preferably give ourselves a reward—a second cup of coffee or a nice biscuit. It might sound trite, but this is a serious point. Providing a reward helps to associate the experience with something positive and strengthens our resolve.

And at the following networking opportunity, we should try to extend ourselves slowly and carefully toward the next milestone.

A successful technique is to think of them as "freeze-dried" goals—just add water and watch them grow!

All we need to do is exercise choice. And start small.

Imposter Buster

Many of us will be familiar with the term "Imposter Syndrome." It's interesting to explore some of the history behind "IS."

The term is actually a corruption of the one used in research that is widely accepted to be the source document. This is a paper authored back in 1978 by Drs. Pauline Rose Clance and Suzanne Imes. Both have a background in well-established Gestalt therapy. Gestalt is a word of German origin that can generally be taken to mean "all"—practitioners look to treat the whole human; mind, body, all.

Some people consider Gestalt to be "the whole is more than the sum of its parts." This could be quite a neat way of thinking about it.

Clance and Imes' original phrase was "Imposter Phenomenon." This just goes to show that even academia and science are not immune to a bit of marketing massaging if it makes something a bit more attractive on the tongue! Anyway, "IP" had already been "taken" in normal parlance as meaning "Intellectual Property." So, it became "IS" or Imposter Syndrome.

The focus of the research covered this question:

Despite outstanding academic and professional accomplishments, women who experience the imposter phenomenon persist in believing that they are really not bright and have fooled anyone who thinks otherwise. (Clance and Imes 1978)

Let's ask ourselves that same question. Have we ever felt that we are not worthy of our current position or pay? Are we simply winging it? And, more to the point, do we have a deep-seated worry that we'll be found out, exposed to our peers and lose everything we have?

If we have ever felt that way, we may be suffering from Imposter Syndrome.

But suffering is a word that invokes feelings. And maybe the word and those feelings need to be challenged?

Far from being something we should try to remedy, recent commentators (including Grant; see the book *Think Again*) have suggested that it may be something that helps us.

How? Well, it might, if approached correctly, force us forward to persevere when we have otherwise given up. It's all a question of how we see it. Is it a pathology, something that needs to be "treated" like an illness, or should we embrace it as a driver to propel us to success?

Everyone experiences self-doubt at one time or another (many of us quite a lot of the time!). There's nothing wrong with this as long as we don't ruminate or wallow in self-pity. Rumination is the process of thinking deeply about something (*Collins English Dictionary* 2005), but in this context to an excessive extent!

So, the message is: "embrace" imposter syndrome. Recognize it for what it is; something that can be genuinely useful if we want to get on in life.

"To be yourself in a world that is constantly trying to make you something else is the greatest accomplishment" (Ralph Waldo Emerson)

Suggested Networking Milestones

- I will attend one networking gathering per week for the next four weeks. I'll write out three specific notes per gathering afterward to reflect on each experience.
- At my next gathering, I will initiate conversation with three people I haven't met before.
- When I next speak with someone for the first time and discover a common interest, I will suggest a one-to-one follow up to talk further. Perhaps a meet up at a coffee shop.
- The next time I'm part of a syndicate break-out at an Annual Conference or similar gathering, I will act as spokesperson for the group and deliver the findings to the room.

The milestone targets should be **SMART**:

- SPECIFIC,
- MEASURABLE,
- ATTRACTIVE (to you, or at least just think of the reward!),
- REALISTIC, and
- TIME-BASED (try not to put things off for too long).

Acknowledging Networking Nerves

We know the feeling. We're due to attend the ultimate face-to-face networking opportunity. Industry leaders from our chosen field will be there. Potential employers will be there.

But there's one thing holding us back. The knot in the pit of our stomach telling us we'll make a complete mess of it, banishing our chances of a successful career (and forever!).

So why don't we give ourselves the perfect recipe to handle the situation and make any nerves work to our advantage?

- Preparation will help to calm nerves. There are lots of tips in the book to help with perfect preparation.
- Tame our inner chimp.

We are outside the venue about to go in. What is known as our "fight or flight" response might start to kick in. Our hearts beat faster, our mouth goes dry.

We can now act to control what the Olympic sports expert, Dr. Steve Peters, calls our "inner chimp." The chimp needs to be told that their services, effectively our evolutionary behaviors intended to protect us from harm, are not required for this situation.

Taking short, gentle breaths from our tummy rather than from our chest will help. This will have the effect of slowing down our respiratory system and relaxing us.

- Nerves are not a negative thing. They can provide us with energy and quite often serve to channel a useful edge, allowing us to raise our game.

  The great theater and film actor, Lord Olivier, was once asked if, after many years on the stage, he still suffered from butterflies. "Of course, I do" he replied, "but these days they fly in formation."
- Reframe and rename. Thinking about the situation in a different way will also help.

  We should ask ourselves "What's the worst that can happen?" Going to a networking event is unlikely to involve us in a life-threatening situation. In the general scheme of things, this single episode will not have a major effect on our life chances. We can remind ourselves that we have done our preparation and done it well. We are ready.

  It can be useful to rename things. If the term "networking" fills us with dread, then we shouldn't refer to it as that. We can rename it "meeting people" or "chatting with others," or any other words that have a positive meaning for us.

- We can consider other people at the event who will be feeling the same way as us. A good tip is for us to focus on what can be done to help *them* feel more comfortable.

  A great example of this is being generous when in a group conversation. If we notice someone standing alone, we can invite them into the group. It's polite, it's friendly, and it will make us feel good!

- If we make a mistake in the presence of others, research shows there is usually only one party that notices it most—ourselves. The best policy is just to continue (perhaps after a short apology if we have made a major social blunder).

- We shouldn't forget the reward. In recognition of all our hard work, we should promise ourselves a treat—perhaps a bar of chocolate. Our evolutionary makeup helps here, as our brains are hardwired to respond positively to reward that is, it makes us perform better.

  We now have a game plan for the next time we are about to attend an event; and we know the more networking we do, the easier it gets.

  It's also important after the event to give ourselves a pat on the back and reflect on the things that went well. We can resolve to do them even better next time.

  This is key as an action to build personal resilience.

  And finally, we can eat that bar of chocolate. We deserve it!

Reflection and Rumination

This is just a short one (you'll be relieved to hear. Ha!).

I've been Googling again. Nasty habit, but there you go …

This time, I've looked at the practice of reflexivity. Or put another way: reflecting, reflexive practice, musing, meditating, contemplating, and so on. Call it what you will.

In the field of Learning and Development, just one of the worlds that I inhabit, this is a must do. It's a hallowed and revered practice, akin to religiosity. Scholars refer to it as being *"embedded in human belief structures."*

Over four million hits later and not for the first time, I have some reservations.

If you are someone like me, who is a hard-core nitpicker and anally retentive weirdo, reflexivity is not such a good thing. Here's why.

Everything has a Yin and Yang. For me, taken to extremes, reflexivity has an evil twin. It's called rumination.

And check out any index of mental health practice, you'll find that rumination is a predictor of poor mental health. In 2013, the largest ever online test into stress at the time undertaken by the BBC's Lab, UK, and the University of Liverpool, England, revealed *"that rumination is the biggest predictor of the most common mental health problems in the country."*

It is also said to be linked to general anxiety, posttraumatic stress, binge drinking, eating disorders, and self-harming. That's quite a list!

So, reflect if you will. Just don't ruminate!

Take Action

- Networking insights can come from anywhere. Practice being open to opportunity.
- Don't be held back by networking myths or limiting beliefs.
- Consider role-playing—Fake It Until You Make It.
- Set modest SMART goals and gradually build on these.
- Build personal rewards into your Strategic Business Networking.
- Exercise choice.
- Reflect to improve performance. But don't ruminate.

CHAPTER 4

Networking as a Process (The Process Play)

If we are starting out on our networking journey, or perhaps wish to take a fresh look at how we do things, it can help to lay down a framework.

To clarify, this is not a prescriptive way to network. As mentioned in the introduction, there will always be different strokes for different folks. But scaffolding knowledge in this way helps as a start point and is particularly useful when it comes to practicing the techniques.

And there's the rub. We must get out and practice.

The good news is the more we do, the easier it will get.

Attending networking events will also bring us into contact with other people who will have their own individual approach to networking. This provides an opportunity to observe and jettison those behaviors that don't fit with our style while adopting, developing, and refining those that do.

There's an adage in face-to-face people networking that says: "If you don't go, you'll never know!" Need we say more?

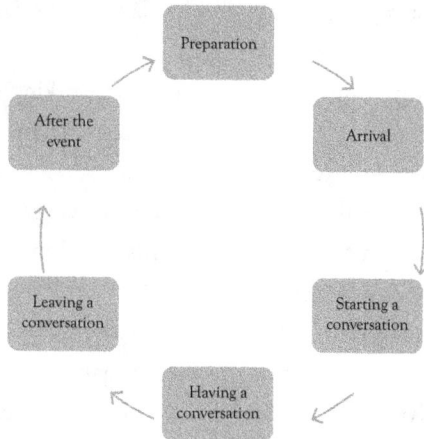

The Strategic Business Networking framework for Face-to-Face Networking Events

The diagram takes us through six stages of what can happen before, during, and after a F2F networking event. It's shown as a self-reinforcing circle, because what we do, say, and learn at one networking gathering should always inform our approach to the events that follow.

Let's concentrate on three stages where experience suggests there is scope for all of us to perform better. We just need to take on board some simple, easy-to-learn techniques.

These are:

- Preparation
- Conversation
- Action immediately after the event.

Preparation (The Be Ready Play)

Let's focus on what really matters under the heading of Preparation:

1. Get ourselves ready, plus any resources we may wish to marshal.
2. Try to find out who is going to be at the event and prepare for small talk.

Getting Ourselves Ready

Here, we could trot out the saying "Fail to plan, plan to fail." But would we be that boring?

Well yes, actually. Going along to a F2F networking event without any thinking in advance is leaving things entirely to chance.

This is fine if we want to take the view that we *might* get lucky. But Strategic Business Networking is about *making sure* we get lucky. If we are going to spend our own time attending events—and most of us do—it's sensible to maximize our effectiveness.

Strategic Business Networking does not leave things to chance. But we may find we need less time to prepare as we gain experience.

Getting ourselves ready means that, initially, we need to get our heads in the right place. We can bring from our toolkit some of the techniques outlined previously, such as setting modest SMART targets, acknowledging nerves, building in rewards, resolving to reflect afterward, and not to ruminate.

As far as resources are concerned, the time-honored tradition of printed business cards hasn't yet been bettered, despite the plethora of apps that allow us to tap our smartphones together or scan QR codes and so on.

A top tip here is to have the card printed on nonglossy paper, with the reverse side blank. Why? Because very many networkers still hold to the practice of making notes on our business cards about who we are, where and when we met, what baseball team we support, and so forth.

And these people are likely, but not exclusively, to be more-experienced hiring managers who have picked up on habits that aren't exactly cutting edge, such as actually writing helpful networking information on pieces of paper. If we have any doubts, we should listen carefully next time we visit the rest room. The sound of scribbling pens may well be heard from any cubicle!

Of course, there will be exceptions. For example, those in hi-tech industries may well use tap-and-go methods and eschew the paper. But the big take home here is for us to think beforehand about the type of event and the cross-section of people who will be there. If we can keep flexible in our approach, we can win the day.

Text on the front of the card needs to be rather like our LinkedIn profile (see the later chapter on social media). Photos can be good as a memory jogger and, on the same theme, something memorable about who we are and what we do. Our LinkedIn "Headline" can be a useful starting point when deciding how to word this.

Explicitly avoiding job titles allows us not to have to explain immediately whether we are in work at present or not. In a way, titles are irrelevant; we are saying what we can bring to the party, not where we rank or ranked in an organization. In any event, many far-sighted organizations have relieved themselves of the burden of titles. This may be a trend we'll see continue in future.

Contact points should be stated for the obvious reason that we need to make it easy for people to get back in touch with us if they want to. Again, we must think about our target audience. If we are networking with journalists and the media, it's appropriate to print our Twitter handle. If it's a collection of homeland security operatives, it might mark us out as loose-tongued. And especially if our Twitter handle is @ slackjaw!

There's another serious point here. These days, it's no great problem to obtain a great professional looking domain name for free or at minimal cost. We need to think about how our e-mail address renders: "squeakybunny@hotmail.com" is unlikely to win professional friends and influence them!

Some events might call for a CV to be prepared and brought along. However, this has a couple of issues. We won't always know who we'll meet and best practice these days is to have a number of different "tweaked" CVs according to the right opportunities. Bringing out the wrong version at the wrong time won't cut the mustard.

And, on the subject of the right time, it may be better to wow your conversational partner with small talk, moving later into professional talk, than have them stand in front of us attempting to read a document that we've just handed them. The CV can always come later.

This is not a book about presentation skills, so it won't be appropriate to go into details about hair, make-up, piercings, or tattoos. And hallelujah to that! We just need to be sensible and dress according to context, if necessary going one level up in dress code as a form of "insurance." In short, dress to impress. As an example for us guys, a necktie can always be covertly removed upon the first trip to the restroom. It's much harder to go find one when the stores are all closed!

Try to Find Out Who Is Going to Be at the Event and Prepare for Small Talk

Researching attendees may require some guile, especially so when some event organizers are understandably guarded over attendee data (and Data Protection law means they have a point). Plus, there is no guarantee that the key contact we wanted to meet will be there.

Even so, if we have access to a list, spending a few minutes Googling will help with our planning, strategy, and influencing.

A solution to the "no attendee lists" problem is to arrive at the event early and undertake a quick sweep of the name badge table. It is always a good idea to say hello to and engage the event organizer. After all, it's in their interests the event goes well so we immediately have a common objective.

We should tell the organizer about ourselves (see later "How to Craft Our Key Messages") and our reasons for attending the event and ask if there is anyone who we should meet. We might even press our case by asking if it might be possible for the host to introduce us personally.

Now let's think about small talk. It's often said that "BIG THINGS come from small talk."

"Small talk" is a vital part of face-to-face interaction. It marks us out as fully paid up members of humanity. Anthropologists, such as Professor Robin Dunbar of the University of Oxford, suggest that small talk (and gossip) is the human equivalent of animals grooming each other in the wild.

Apes in the wild ...

Image © 2021 Daniel Byron

There's an assumption that grooming in animals involves catching fleas. But free-living monkeys don't have that many fleas and skin parasites (these tend to multiply in different, more confined conditions).

Rather, when monkeys groom, they are mostly removing items caught in fur, or scabs and other skin blemishes. It involves a gentle teasing and tugging—much more like subtle massage than anything else. This promotes an endorphin release associated with pleasurable feelings. So maybe there's more to human conversation than meets the eye!

When we first start a conversation with someone new, it's helpful to have an idea about how to keep things flowing. This way, potentially embarrassing silences and conversational dead ends can be avoided.

This is where preparation comes in. So that we have something in our kit bag, we should try researching in advance some simple but interesting facts about:

- The speaker (and there normally is one). What is their background? What are their specialist topics? Have they recently said anything of note?
- The venue and surrounding location. We could do some research on the local area. What are the points of interest? What about the history of the venue itself? When was it built? Who owns it?
- The speaker's subject. Is it topical? Does it raise an interesting question? What view do we have? (This is important. While avoiding anything too contentious, it's acceptable to show that we are our own person and do hold a view. Indeed, important contacts including potential employers may be on the lookout for this).

But we should be careful if there are any political or socially sensitive aspects to the speaker's subject. Better to err on the cautious side until our new contacts get to know us.

Conversation (The Discourse Play)

We'll break this down into three components:

- Starting a Conversation,
- Having a Conversation, and
- Leaving a Conversation.

Starting a Conversation

So, let's assume we have done some preparation, we've arrived at the event and have settled ourselves with a drink and some nibbles.

Another attendee has approached us, or we have approached them. We have greeted each other with a warm smile, introduced ourselves by name, and shaken hands. What next?

Networking specialists often dispense the advice of an opening question based on the old "Do you come here often?"

While this question may not be at the top of our list, there are other versions that are perfectly adequate such as "What brings you here today (or this evening etc.)?"

Another technique involves the exchange of business cards. There's a temptation often to simply pocket the card and move on. But if a little time is taken to read what is printed on the card this can open up valuable conversation topics, such as the home state or location of the individual and their office.

It can also be useful to employ the mnemonic "JIFFY" to signpost possible topics of conversation. This stands for Jobs, Interests, Family, Friends, and finally, You.

The "You" at the end is intended to signify that this is an opportunity to give the other person the stage. We can think of it as their turn to be in the spotlight. In effect, we are acting as a prompter to keep the conversation flowing.

Of course, it's appropriate to also talk about ourselves at some stage. But be measured in doing so and show some generosity, such as avoiding interruptions when the conversational partner is in full flow.

We can also consider using the technique of reflecting. This involves responding to the comments made by the other party, in effect signaling them to expand upon their theme. Quite often it just requires repetition of the last word said, as in this example:

Partner: Yes, we're just back from holiday ...

Us: Holiday?

Partner: Oh, a beautiful little place, perfect for the children ...

Us: Children?

Partner: Yes, we have three Jemima, Jack, and Jeremy?

Us: Oh really, what age are they?

And so on …

Notice we don't overdo the reflecting, otherwise, it can start to sound false and parrot like.

Nonetheless, reflecting is useful to keep things ticking along to avoid a conversational dead end and can also gather valuable personal information.

In the previous example, if we were to meet this person again, it would be perfectly acceptable to recall that they'd recently been on holiday. In doing so, we'd effortlessly pick up the small talk part of any conversation where we left off. We have a ready-made conversation starter for next time.

Next, let's talk about names.

Names are important. After introductions have been made, we'll generally know if we are in the company of an accomplished networker if they mention our given name maybe three or four times early in the conversation.

Two things are happening here. First, this is a memory piece on the part of the person repeating the name. They are locking it into long-term memory.

If this doesn't seem important, we should consider how often influential and successful people are described as having a good memory for names and being capable of greeting people personally many years after the first introduction. It's a very powerful tool.

Secondly, names are personal. Supported by our parent or caregiver, we learn our name as young children, possibly as one of the very first words we assimilate.

The point is that the capacity for associating one's name with formative events is strong. Ask any school teacher and they will tell us that knowing the names of the students in their class and being able to quote them with ease, gives them a degree of influence and authority.

Hence using someone's name always carries a personal angle, which is useful for building rapport quickly with someone we've only just met.

So, we should try the technique of repeating someone's name after the initial introduction and early in the conversation. It might sound strange the first few times we do it but, after practice, it will come more naturally and be invaluable in aiding the memory and building the relationship.

These techniques are preferable to dominating the conversation with our own angle on JIFFY, while the other half of the interaction looks on in bewildered silence. Behave this way and we'll probably find ourselves alone quite quickly!

There has been a significant amount of research around the proportion of conversation between two people to promote an effective networking interaction. Some say 80/20, others say 70/30 (the smaller number refers to our contribution).

It may be more about our basic needs as human beings. And a wish to be heard and understood.

That's why it can be important to tell our story, but only after giving time and space to the other party, thereby allowing them to tell theirs. Some commentators refer to this as a kind of verbal "dance" and this seems to be a pretty good way of looking at it.

We'll realize very soon if the pendulum swings too far. A conversation under these conditions ceases to be genuinely two-way and instead turns into a lecture!

Having a Conversation

With the ice broken, the coast is normally clear to enter deeper conversation.

This could include more about what the other person does and enough information for us to judge whether an opportunity element to the conversation can be introduced.

For example, are there mutually beneficial opportunities that fit with our own strategy? Or perhaps we can assist the other person with information, advice, or guidance from our knowledge and experience?

This isn't about pressing a sale or going in for the kill. We should be wary of jumping the gun and engaging in what Dr. Ivan Misner (founder and Chairman of business networking organization BNI) calls "premature solicitation"!

On the other hand, let's be clear. Networking events usually happen because of an implicit theme of commerce and business relationship building. Business-talk is part of the scene.

It's also perfectly legitimate to consider that any hiring managers who are present at the event might be in talent recruitment mode.

Moving into business mode also requires preparation and forethought. The aim should be to provide a coherent story of where we've come from, where we are now, and in what direction we hope to go forward.

There's more about this in the later chapter, "How to Craft Our Key Messages."

Leaving a Conversation

This part of the dialogue normally raises a smile. It's probably because most of us have experienced that slightly unsettling interaction with someone who will just not leave us alone.

Picture the scene. There tends to be only two people left in the conversational group. We've introduced ourselves to the other party and what has followed is a reasonable discussion about jobs, interests, family, and friends.

But there has been a dawning realization on our part: Although a pleasant conversation, it's unlikely the relationship will develop much more. And the other party may feel the same about us.

For any readers who might be uncomfortable with the blunt tone of the last paragraph, we should remind ourselves of our initial premise. Our networking time is scarce. Unless we are strategic in approaching how we behave, we can spend a lot of time doing the right things in the wrong way.

We are not saying that we should treat other people as we would a disposable tissue, once we decide they can be of no use. Potentially, everyone and anyone might be able to provide counsel and advice at some point in our lives.

However, we can't work on unfounded assumptions based on the far long term (unless we have limitless time to network). Therefore, strategic decisions need to be made while always, of course, treating people with the respect and dignity that we would expect ourselves.

So, how can we exit gracefully once a conversation has run its course? How do we know when a conversation has reached this point? Sometimes, like leaves in the fall, we just know.

First, it's a good idea to give ourselves permission. We have come to the event to network with everyone there, not to spend all evening with one person. We owe it to ourselves to gain the best value from our time. Being kind to ourselves is just as important as being kind to others.

After waiting for an appropriate gap in the conversation, we can exit with the following:

"It's been great speaking with you but:

... I need to go and refresh my drink."

... I need to go to the restroom." (Hoping they don't follow us!)

... we're both here to network, so I'll move on around the room."

Some experienced networkers offer the advice of never leaving our conversational partner on their own. It's suggested that they be introduced to another contact, associate, or friend. But that person may not thank us for this later!

A better alternative would be to direct them to the host (we will have contacted the host earlier and know them by name). They have responsibility for all guests. We can provide a short intro, before moving away.

Other times a good measure can be when the conversation has become circular. In other words, we arrive back at a topic we discussed earlier in the conversation. This always provides a natural hiatus. We pause for breath and probably the next few words should be something like:

- "I really should circulate; it's been great meeting you!" or,
- "It's a networking event, so perhaps we should network! Great to meet you!" or,
- "Gosh, it's a little warm in here, I should refresh my glass. Can I get you a drink while I'm there?"

Author's note: It's often very warm at networking events: it's all that hot air! When you return with the drinks, you can take your exit then if appropriate. But, sometimes, there's a new person who has joined your former conversational partner. Wow, a whole new person you can be introduced to and who you can network with!

Action Immediately After the Event (The Follow-Up Play)

Following up after the event can sometimes be hard to do.

It's perhaps a human failing, but we really don't like to risk being judged and/or suffer rejection. Some have even suggested that the emotion of fear comes into play.

But we must do it.

Here are some follow-up actions:

- If we promised to call, do so,
- If we promised to e-mail with our full contact details, do so,
- If we promised to send a link to an interesting article we referred to, do so,
- If we promised to connect with them on LinkedIn, do so (but let's make sure we use a personalized, nonstandard invitation).

With every interaction we should proceed with a degree of caution. Don't rush. And we should be thinking of three things:

1. Briefly remind the recipient of the context; for example, where we met them, what was said. We shouldn't assume they will remember us!

2. Have a key point that we want to get across. Make the point clearly and succinctly. If it involves a question or request, once this has been asked STOP AND WAIT. This is a key technique known to all master influencers. We need to give the respondent the time and space to reply. If we gabble on after we've made a request, we may cause the opportunity to be lost.

3. Point the way forward. Gently and respectfully state what we'd like to happen next (e.g., meet up for coffee to continue the discussion). Sometimes, the act of asking a polite question in the final paragraph of our note can help to promote engagement and prompt a reply. This isn't being pushy. It's about taking the initiative. And actively demonstrating our potential and worth as a future contact or employee.

Our Strategic Business Networking strategy should include continually moving the relationship forward to the next interaction; for example, from networking event to telephone call, to coffee meeting, to in-office discussion (which may well turn into an informal job interview or sales opportunity).

Failing to follow up undoes all the hard work carried out in the preparation and small talk stages.

People can have short memories and the working day can be long and stressful. If we don't follow up quickly and effectively, we and our proposal will be forgotten.

There's another important point. Doing what we said we'd do has scientific underpinning.

The "Big 5" personality factors are often expressed by the mnemonic "OCEAN." This stands for:

- Openness to new experience,
- Conscientiousness,
- Extraversion,
- Agreeableness, and
- Neuroticism.

And here's the secret sauce: it's being conscientious that research identifies as the best predictor of success in a job. The other factors have a part to play, but conscientiousness stands out.

And the beauty of following up is that it offers tangible proof of our conscientiousness to any important networking contact or potential employer. It's a demonstration that we can be trusted to do what we say we'll do.

To quote the words of the former UK Government Minister and businessman, Lord Young of Graffham, we should "Focus and follow through."

Pointing the Way Forward

Many networkers seem to stumble at this point. I'm not sure why. It's really just a process of being helpful to the reader.

As discussed earlier, the final paragraph of any written communication should point the way forward. Marketeers call this a "Call to Action." It's a statement that directs the reader to what they should do next (and even, sometimes, when and how they should do it!).

As an example, in the Internet age, we are all familiar with being asked to "Buy Now" or "Click Here." The advertising industry also knows all about this; for example, Nike's well-known slogan: Just Do It!

I would avoid issuing an instruction to the recipient. Instead, make the language softer but still keep it as a call to action:

"… if it works for you, I'll give you a call tomorrow"

or

"… if you are free, let's meet next week for coffee"

Or we might say something like

"Look forward to seeing you next week as I promised to discuss your banking with you"

or

"I'll send over that interesting paper I mentioned."

It's not a strict rule, but a call to action can work both ways. Something that we want someone else to do, or confirmation of something that we will do.

We should finish with a thank you. This is important, if only because so many people forget to do this. If they are dumb enough to forget, no problem, we'll capitalize on our advantage and stand out from the crowd.

Take Action

- For F2F events, to start with, consider using the Strategic Business Networking framework and always employ the Prepare stage beforehand.
- BIG things come from small talk.
- Having a conversation: try JIFFY, reflecting, names.
- Don't make it all about you. Give way to conversational space.
- Give yourself permission to leave a conversation.
- Follow up. Follow up. Follow up (have I said that enough?).

CHAPTER 5

Getting the Message Across (The Bongs Play)

Before we consider constructing our message, it's worth looking at research around communication and how we as humans communicate best.

This is important. Let's assume we have carefully crafted a message about who we are, what we do, and our desired direction of career travel.

We may have labored long and hard to create this.

But if we don't communicate the message in the right way, all our efforts will be wasted. Our approach should not just be about message transmission but also successful message reception.

And the latter has a lot to do with how humans process sensory information. This includes the sounds we make, in addition to things such as how we look and other, nonverbal cues.

Tapping In

When interacting with other people in a networking context, we need to be able to communicate quickly and clearly who we are and what it is we do (and, in the case of career development, what it is we want to do).

Here's a quick experiment from Adam Grant's book "Originals." This can be tried in the company of a friend, family member, or work colleague.

First, we need to think of a familiar melody. It can be anything— Chart Top 40, nursery rhyme, classical, whatever.

Then, in the presence of the friend, we tap out the rhythm of the song. No singing, no humming, just tapping. As this is done, the friend must guess the title of the song.

As straightforward as this may seem, this can turn out to be quite a challenging communication exercise.

When formal research was conducted at Stanford University (Newton, 1990), people were first asked to estimate whether the song would be named correctly. Participants generally thought it would be easy and predicted that a correct guess would be made more than 50 percent of the time. In fact, only 2.5 percent of people guessed accurately.

So, what's going on here? Surely, if we can hear a melody in our head it shouldn't be that difficult to communicate this to a third party?

The answer lies in our human tendencies. Overall, we are an over-confident bunch. And we could say there might be good evolutionary reasons for this. For example, if we didn't believe that we could fight the saber tooth tiger and win, we might just as well sit at the back of the cave and shiver!

This overconfidence also applies to our attempts at communication. In the tapping exercise, we hear the song in our heads and find it hard to believe the other person can't hear it in the same way.

Similarly, when meeting people for the first time, we have our perfect message clear in our heads. We assume it must be equally clear to them. And we find it very hard to conceive they won't be able to understand it in the same way that we do.

It's all about "the Bongs"

King Kong knows …

Image © 2021 Daniel Byron

So, what has this got to do with career management and developing people networks?

Whether we are engaging with a new contact at a networking event, we need to have a quick and catchy reply to the question "… and what do you do?"

It's imperative that we then have a second version to emphasize the point, followed by a third to really ensure the message is embedded. It's an approach that builds gradually on our story and avoids misunderstanding.

It allows time for the messages to be processed by the recipient. In addition, by having slightly different versions on the same theme, if the first message fails to hit its target there is an excellent chance the second or third version will hit home.

The principle can be demonstrated through the story of a senior TV executive involved in the production of the UK's Independent Television late-evening flagship programme, News at Ten.

Her professional take on communication is that it is "all about the bongs." This is a reference to News at Ten's established practice of having the chime (or "bong") of Big Ben precede each news story.

Her approach was to handle each story in chunks of 5 seconds, 15 seconds, and 60 seconds. "Chunking" is a well-known technique to deliver complex information effectively as an aid to cognition. It refers to breaking down messages into small, digestible parcels.

The first five seconds of the news item is the bong! This acts as a vital attention grabber and is followed by a short headline. (It's also interesting to note that the songs of Led Zeppelin, by anyone's standards one of the most successful bands in the history of rock music, invariably start with a loud attention-grabbing guitar riff. They are difficult to miss!)

The next 15-second chunk is a headline repeat but varied and extended slightly. This second version is important to keep the viewer engaged— particularly so if the meat of the story is scheduled for the following half of the program, after a commercial break.

The final 60-second slot, sometimes slightly longer, is a headline re-repeat and the story in detail.

This approach guarantees that both the content and flavor of the communication catches the attention and comes across clearly to the TV audience.

Similarly, our detailed message to a new contact needs the same gradual approach, each version building upon the former.

There is no point our hammering out a long-winded explanation, hardly pausing for breath. Under these conditions, our message won't be received adequately and much less likely understood.

If we allow time for messages to be processed, we'll stand a much better chance of receiving that all-important feedback from our recipient—a question. Them asking a question often denotes interest and indicates that our transmission has been successful.

We are also well on the way to another by-product of efficient communication: being memorable.

In the context of memorability and networking practice, a mantra of Andy Lopata's is appropriate. Labeled "Mr. Networking" by UK's *The Sun* newspaper, Andy's words ring true:

"If you want someone to remember you, you need to be in their head—not just in their business card holder!"

The next chapter looks at being memorable in more detail and considers how to craft the messages that underpin our communications.

How to Get People to Remember You? (Clance and Imes revisited, gender politics, and should you avoid taboos?)

Bear with me please. I first need to explain where I'm coming from.

When researching this book, I thought it only sensible to take a look at the Clance and Imes paper in the original (see "Imposter Buster" earlier). What I found surprised me.

I should first provide some context: I consider myself primarily a social psychologist. I've always been interested in the individual and the stories we tell ourselves. For me, context matters. I believe that how humans behave depends to a large extent on their surroundings and circumstances (notice how I've just said "I should first provide some context"—it's important to me!).

I remember choosing a topic for my master's dissertation. My background is finance and it's therefore no surprise that I'm quite good with numbers—I score relatively highly on arithmetic reasoning tests (probably both nature and nurture at work here).

All of this should have led me to undertake a quantitative study for my dissertation; crunching numbers on large datasets and producing graphs and tables to assert how my results could be generalized to apply to the whole population. Brilliant!

But, I decided to do what I thought would be a much more interesting study involving a relatively small sample size and take a qualitative route. My study involved interviewing five (yes, only five!) people about their experiences of working from home—and then drawing some conclusions about what they had said and how they said it. How prescient of me in 2010!

A super intelligent and very helpful peer tried to convince me otherwise: "*Darryl, why the heck are you doing a Qual study? You are so much better suited to Quant—you're really good at it!*"

Researchers who are pure quant can be a little dismissive of these methods. It's understandable, they cannot see for the life of them how the research results can be generalized (it's just people waffling on after all!) and they certainly don't consider a participant sample in single figures to be anywhere near representative. If pushed, they might play the pseudo-science card and suggest that my research is nothing more than complete piffle.

The thing is, as far as I can see, Clance and Imes interviewed 172 women (bigger than my sample, but still very small by Quant standards). Furthermore, the paper prints to just over 8 sides of A4 and cites only 7 papers within the References section (I had a list of 74 for my very undistinguished MSc paper!).

So what point am I trying to make? Well, the paper has been very influential for something so short. It is, of course, "of its time." I count myself a feminist but the paper does, by my reading, take issue with men as a species. And perhaps unnecessarily so, although it is clear to say that "men who appear to be more in touch with their feminine qualities" are susceptible to IS.

It also says the IS phenomenon "occurs with much less frequency in men and that, when it does occur, it is with much less intensity."

I am not looking for a gender politics debate, but these words feel to me to be slightly demeaning of "men" because they imply a category. My life experience is that many people of the male gender experience imposter syndrome. I'm not aware that it is any less intense. And I'm one of them.

To their credit, later researchers have taken up these topics.

How is it for you?

Author's note: *"Qualitative treatment of data describes what processes are occurring and details differences in the character of these processes over time. In contrast, a quantitative treatment states what the processes are, how often they occur, and what differences in their magnitude can be measured over time"* (Breakwell et al. 2008).

Of course, what I should have done is a mixed methods study giving me the best of both worlds thereby receiving the aplomb of both camps. In reality, qual and quant distinctions are what my old undergrad lecturer would call an "unhelpful binary" and, as divisive terms, best avoided. Putting it bluntly, they are just "two cheeks from the same butt." Again!

A prologue. And an important message to you:

I've been slightly political here with my comments. I don't mean to be so. And I certainly don't want to invite hate mail or social media trolling.

I want to make two important points:

First, the old networking adage says, "Never discuss subjects that are taboo."

But you know what? There's something about the slow, and some say pernicious, impact of social media, which I think has changed this well-established maxim.

We all realize that, on social media, people are so much more ready to express opinions. The medium encourages it. Sometimes with disastrous results!

But, and it's a big but, perhaps a more positive slant is that we are slowly becoming less offended by and more inured to others voicing an opinion. Whether we feel it's the right one or not. After all, they are entitled to it and, in the right context, also entitled to express it.

So maybe we could, in our networking conversations, judiciously move into what would hitherto have been considered slightly tricky waters.

I'm not suggesting that we immediately go up to someone who we know to be a Yankees supporter and tell them proudly of our affiliation to the Red Sox. That would be social capital hara-kiri.

But maybe we could, in our networking conversations, judiciously move into what would hitherto have been considered very dangerous waters indeed. Just by taking a calculated chance.

This "play" could be particularly effective where we might need, for reasons of timing, to move the relationship forward at speed.

So maybe social media is currently getting a bad rap. But it's not all bad, is it?

The second point is much less a discussion and more by way of guidance to you.

Clance and Imes wrote an academic paper, which is not the most comprehensive and wordy in the known universe. But it took off!

Or rather, it took off when others became part of the movement and even changed the name of the subject from "Imposter Phenomenon" to "Imposter Syndrome."

Why did this happen? How did this happen?

The people networking take home is that clever marketing (and replacing the word "phenomenon" with "syndrome" *is* clever marketing) needs to be applied to any good idea.

Having a good idea alone, particularly in a modern information-overload world, is just not enough. You need to find some traction to get the message out there and have others repeat it, thereby winning supporters.

And, Abra Cadabra!, Hey Presto!* a movement is formed to which people feel attracted. A sense of belonging is engendered, much as in the same way we can feel affiliation to our families and friends.

If you can become someone who is seen to be at the center of a worthy movement, or near to it, you will find that people are attracted to you by association.

So go out there and do good. It will feel good, and people will love you for it.

* These days, no book is complete without a reference to Harry Potter. Harry, I'm told, says "Avada Kedavra." Some say this means "I destroy as I speak." In contrast, "Abra Kadabra" from ancient Aramaic is said to mean "I create as I speak." This is the root of our modern "Abra Cadabra."

The accompanying "Hey Presto" is generally taken to mean "as if by magic." The root here is a musical direction—"Presto: At a rapid tempo."

Notice how both these terms tend to be said in a loud stage voice. It's the same principle as The Bongs outlined earlier. The magician is calling the audience to attention.

Take Action

- What we say isn't necessarily what people hear.
- We need something to grab the attention. In a networking context, this usually involves saying something that piques the interest of our new conversational partner. But many TV presenters or celebrities do it through what they wear; whether this is a "loud" neck tie, or, in the case of Lady Gaga, clothing fashioned from raw meat!
- If you want someone to remember you, you need to be in their head.
- Find a worthy cause and work hard at it. Attract people through association. Pull is easier than push.

CHAPTER 6

How to Craft Our Key Messages (The Who, Why, and What Play)

Let's assume we've moved beyond the small talk stage. We know a little about the social life of our conversational partner and they know a little about ours. We're on first name terms.

As we've seen in the last chapter, we're now ready to go deeper in terms of conversation and content. It's an opportunity for us to take the spotlight and say something about who we are.

This is another area that is all too easy to leave to chance. Some networkers will attempt to "wing it" and hope they find the right words for the occasion. Others think that the planning of messages leaves things too scripted.

Strategic Business Networking disagrees. It recommends careful analysis of our own value proposition and the detailed crafting of messages. These should support a compelling proposition that states, "We can be a valued contact, consultant, or employee."

Let's be clear. In a networking situation, we are very much in the mode of selling ourselves. We need to have a good understanding of what our "product" features, advantages, and benefits are, and how we can best articulate them.

And articulate them well enough to burn in the memory of our conversation partner—because being memorable is a prime objective.

The key highlights of these messages need to be learned. In this way, they are ready at hand and capable of being employed when opportunity strikes.

It would be great if we could come up with a magic formula to help everyone determine their key messages.

Unfortunately, it isn't that simple. What we have to offer is invariably as unique as the individual. No two people are exactly alike. And, for the best possible reasons, only the individual can get to the heart of what they do and even why they do it.

It takes work to answer these questions, but the good news is that some pointers are to hand to help us figure things out.

Hints and Tips

To dissect our message, let's consider three areas. These build on the very valuable work of Joshua Waldman, founder of "Career Enlightenment":

1. Who are you?
2. Why are you the best?
3. What kind of work are you looking for?

1. Who Are You?

This question is usually the shorthand answer to the usual "and what do you do?" networking question. This really means "Please give me a short, succinct description which I can understand and process easily. Oh, and make it memorable if you can."

We could say:

"I'm an analyst for an investment bank"

or

"I'm an accountant."

In both cases, the problem is we would simply be parroting our job titles. And job titles are poor indicators of what we do or the value we bring to an organization.

Simple titles can also have the effect of sparking "schemas" within the listener. Schemas are internal models of how we categorize the world around us. They are a kind of cognitive shorthand to make daily life easier for our brains.

But they carry a risk. The unintended consequence of describing ourselves simply as an accountant is that we are lumped into the "accountant file" within the listener's internal model—whether we fit it or not.

As such, we stand little chance of differentiating ourselves from how all the other accountant acquaintances have been categorized. And it's highly unlikely we'll stand out in any way.

Here are some alternative replies in each case:

"I work with numbers and help link data to the important decisions made by our investment bank fund managers."

Or:

"I help businesspeople get behind the figures in their financial reports. This makes them better managers."

In both cases, we are keeping the initial reply tight and succinct. But we are also hinting at the practical effect of what we do and hence the value we bring (better decisions, better managers).

These types of statements always carry more interest than bland job descriptions. They also ratchet up the chance that our conversation partner will pick up on the message and ask a question in follow up. And interest, together with individual meaning (what psychologists call salience), are great at binding the memory.

Another good approach to get to the root of our value proposition is the "So what?" question. This is a variation on a technique taught by global negotiation specialist, Derek Arden.

Here's how it works.

First, we need to think again of ourselves as a product or service. Then, ask ourselves:

"What's the product of the product?" (e.g., what's the real outcome of what I do?)

Or

"What's the difference that makes the difference?" (e.g., what is it about what I do that has an impact?)

The next stage, once we have an answer to these questions is to ask, "So what?" In effect, we are self-questioning our responses.

We can carry on with the "So what?" question until we feel we have exhausted it and can go no further.

At this point, we are probably very close to the essence of what we do.

As a very useful by-product, we'll also have a greater understanding of *why* we do it and what it means to us. We start to recognize how what we do makes us feel.

Thinking is not the same as feeling. Thoughts can be justified, critiqued, examined, or maybe even attacked. Whereas feelings "just are."

And tapping into these "feeling" aspects can be very useful.

Social scientists agree that human decisions are invariably made based on "feel" rather than the cold, hard logic that we mistakenly believe has the upper hand.

If we articulate our worth in the form of what our role means to us, it can also have a very strong impact on others. This includes others in the position of making decisions that might involve us.

It's as if the meaning element is contagious. People wake up to who we really are.

They also remember us better. This is because they can more easily recall not who we are, but *how we made them feel* when they met us.

Powerful stuff!

(If we need convincing further, there are some great examples in Simon Sinek's TED talk "How Great Leaders Inspire Action"—over 55 million viewers can't be wrong!)

2. Why Are You the Best?

It's a competitive market out there. It's, therefore, a good idea to have some content in our conversations to demonstrate our unique qualities.

If we need some assistance with this, a bit of visualization can sometimes help.

Think, when were we at our best? It doesn't have to be a business example. We might call to mind a situation within our personal, community, or family lives.

We could try naming our biggest success. What role did we play? What are we most proud of?

Just getting our thinking in this mode can help in answering the question, "Why are you the best?"

Many of us can find talking about ourselves something of a challenge. Maybe we are quiet in our nature and would rather not toot our own horn.

It's accepted that different people have different personality characteristics. It's a sobering thought that research also identifies a key difference between extraverts and introverts when it comes to communication and influencing.

In general, people overestimate the cognitive abilities of extraverts. Extraverts tend to be able to articulate their thoughts well to influence and persuade.

Those of a more introverted nature are not similarly blessed. The result is the reasoning skills and general intelligence of introverts are often underestimated by others.

Of course, we are talking about extremes. No one is completely extraverted or introverted (Carl Jung, who first coined these words, was against classifying people in this way). In fact, it's estimated that two-thirds of the population are "'ambiverts"—a mixture of the two.

It comes back to making a choice. If we do find it difficult to talk about ourselves, we need to consider trying on a different role and slowly, carefully practicing and developing that skill.

There's another aspect. Culturally, it can be difficult to talk about one's own virtues; society might frown upon it—although some cultures seem to have absolutely no difficulty with it at all!

Recognizing this as an issue and one that we need to develop a strategy for, there's a chapter later in the book on Building Mentor and Advocate Networks. Here we'll talk about the dos and don'ts of bragging.

So, the first area was Who are you? and the second Why are you the best? Now, here's the third area.

3. What Kind of Work (Or Client, If Self-Employed) Are You Looking For?

From a career development viewpoint, we need to give others a sense of our direction of travel. What have we done, where are we now, and where are we headed?

But here's the problem. We sometimes want to spread the net as widely as possible to maximize our chances of finding a new employer or client. In our attempt to catch all, we can mistakenly position ourselves as a kind of Swiss Army knife. Name it, and we can do it!

But this doesn't work, and it would certainly be a handicap in terms of memorability and standing out.

We can't be "all things to all people." We must think about a specialization.

This means starting with an area where we can showcase our expertise, and which allows us to speak enthusiastically about our experiences.

Best-selling author and the name behind "Poised for Partnership," Heather Townsend, talks of becoming the "go to" person within a selective niche.

If we can differentiate from the competition and position ourselves in a memorable way, we can really have an impact on those we meet.

International public speaker Susan Luke Evans has a great phrase: "Pick your lane!"

Additional Hints and Tips

Here are some additional tips that professional networkers have found useful in crafting their messages:

Storytelling

We should try to weave what we say into a coherent story. All stories have a start, middle, and end. So, for example, we could start with some brief scene setting. Then we could move on to the "meat" of what we want to say. After this, we could finish with a recap of what we are about.

We can think of this as a kind of verbal "bullet point." This plays neatly to the "All about the bongs" example of News at Ten.

It also recognizes years of psychological research which demonstrates that, when humans are presented with information, "primacy and recency" applies.

This means that we are biased toward remembering the first thing we experience in a sequence and the last thing. We tend to remember very little in-between.

As such, we should be sure that our priority information is contained within those slots—first and last.

Alliteration, Rhyme, and the Rule of Three

It's a good idea to try some alliteration when telling our story. This is when a series of words in a row or close together have the same first letter sound. For example, "Peter Piper Picked a Peck of Pickled Peppers."

This doesn't mean that we quote tongue twisters in our conversation!

Let's think of Heather Townsend's "Poised for Partnership" example. The phrase rolls off the tongue. Similarly, business intelligence specialist, Julia Hobsbawm, talks of "Names Not Numbers"—a great example of alliterative copywriting.

There's something about these word collections that binds the memory. This may be an evolutionary relic from our communal storytelling past.

Rhyme is also a great tool for making messages stick.

Advertisers know this very well. If we ask ourselves the question "Beans means …," hopefully, most of us would recall the slogan and (importantly) the name of the advertiser as Heinz.

Again, it's not a question of forcing a limerick into our message. But an accountant might describe themselves as a "numbers ninja," a lawyer as a "legal eagle" or we might refer to the social dread of business gatherings as a "networking nightmare."

We spoke of schemas as a form of cognitive efficiency. The Rule of Three is similar. It recognizes our limited short-term capacity to hold information and therefore chunks it up into three segments.

Politicians know the rule very well and employ it regularly. Consider the U.S. Declaration of Independence:

"Life, liberty and the pursuit of happiness."

So, if we want to be understood and our message needs to be made less complex, expressing the message in the form of "A and B, then C" will help.

Alliteration, rhyme, and the Rule of Three are all very useful communication tools. (See what we did there!)

Analogy

If we are having trouble explaining ourselves, it can sometimes help to provide an example from a completely different sphere and then make the comparison.

It's amazing how often this can turn on a lightbulb in people's minds. When this happens, it's always very clear from the reaction we get, and the penny suddenly drops.

One example from the commercial world is the story of business turn-around specialists. Experts in their field, they take on the management of problem companies and literally "turn them around" to profitability.

But the very detailed and specific nature of their work makes it difficult for them to explain clearly exactly what they do. Apart from this, client confidentiality means it is impossible to quote specific examples by way of illustration.

In Association Football (Soccer), the rules allow for players to be substituted during the game. The strategy behind player substitutions in sport would merit a whole new book!

Certain footballers have become known for their skill in coming onto the field of play late in the game and making a significant difference to the outcome of the game. They may provide a valuable "assist" or even score a goal themselves. They are impact players or "Super Subs."

Turnaround specialists can usefully describe their role as a kind of "Super Sub." This way, they get their message across quickly and clearly to a general audience familiar with the normal use of the football term.

Upping Our Elvis

We'll have gathered by now, that conversation can be very nuanced. That's to say that delicate changes in environment and context can make the same phrase or question a winner, or a complete "get me out of here" moment.

Anthropologists know about this stuff and give it several monikers. They would say that language is a cultural tool, and, like most general-purpose tools, it can be used in different ways. A hammer can both drive in nails and pull them out (if it's a claw head hammer).

Now, when we get down into the nitty gritty of an industry or occupation, we know there are certain words that are generally understood in the profession, but are not known in the same way by the general public.

An example? For most people, Campari is a drink often enjoyed with soda. But for a banker in the profession of lending money, "CAMPARI" is a mnemonic to help remember the key questions to be posed to any borrower before they part with the cash!

So, "campari" means something to one group of people and something else to another.

Development of a kind of secret language is useful. If we know what it is and, more importantly, how and when to use it, we can draw our conversational partner closer to us. And, as we have seen before and shall discuss again later, pull is always stronger than push (see "The Importance Play/the Importance *of* Play").

It's useful therefore to think about terms, names, phrases, and so on that are somewhat unique to our industry, trade, or profession. Because using these in the right context can be very useful. You become known for "speaking the right language."

A Secret Society. Or a Society With Secrets— "wordplay" and insider jargon matters

I'm a big fan of YouTube and I follow lots of different channels. I'm also keen on playing and repairing guitars. One channel I follow is that of @Twoodford, which deals with guitar repair and all other things guitar-related.

Ted is a Canadian luthier (a repairer of stringed instruments, mainly guitars) who has developed quite a tribe following.

This is mainly because he is very, very good at his job and an absolute mine of useful information. But he also has personality and a brilliant sense of humor. I suspect the latter is the real attraction for those of us who follow him.

Anyhow, for Ted's followers, the phrase "Kung Fu neck set" is a given—but I wouldn't recommend trying to say it after a couple of glasses of wine!

When a guitar gets old, its action (the height of the strings above the guitar fretboard) can cause problems. In particular, it makes the instrument harder to play. There are various quick-fix ways to address this, but they are usually only delaying the day of judgment.

The only more permanent fix is to reset the angle of the guitar neck with the guitar body. As this joint is made at the point of manufacture and rarely torn asunder, it can be a big job to undertake a "neck set." Plus, it requires specialist tools.

Ted has developed a shortened, but no less effective, method of resetting the neck of a guitar. He, and we followers in his tribe, all know this as "The Kung Fu neck set."

Now you know it too!

Take Action

- How we make people feel is powerful.
- We can choose to sing our own praises. There's nothing to say we can't do this.
- Storytelling and copywriting skills make our verbal and written messages more memorable.
- Use analogy as shorthand to explain what you do and the impact you can have.
- Insider knowledge includes using insider language. Get in with the "in-crowd."

CHAPTER 7

Moving Around a Room (The Dunbar's Number Play)

Of course, the context will vary, but a good many networking events take place in traditional meeting room venues. For this reason, it's useful to look at this setting and how to manage our behavior within it.

As we enter the room we may be met with a range of sensations. Bright lights, background muzak, aromas from the catering station, or the clink of coffee cups or glasses.

Sometimes, this can feel a little overpowering. It's important therefore to take a few moments to settle in and find our feet.

One excellent tip is to head to the drinks station. This has two benefits; a chance to survey the scene and secondly, being in a queue for refreshment is often an opportunity to strike up an impromptu conversation. This gives us a ready-made chance to flex our vocal cords and try out our small talk repertoire.

In the early stages of a social gathering, people tend not to form large conversational groups. Things haven't quite warmed up enough at this stage (unless of course, they already know each other).

The effect of this is that, by arriving early, the challenges of joining a preexisting group don't arise.

For this reason, many networking commentators recommend early arrival. This provides an opportunity to have one-on-one conversations as other guests arrive after and join us, rather than we join them.

Approaching Groups

But even arriving early won't inoculate us from the need at some point to approach a group of people who are having a conversation together.

Let's consider the following four groupings, both in terms of numbers and the respective positions of those conversing.

Group 1

Group 2

Group 3

X X
X

Group 4

X X
X

Conversational groupings

Image © Strategic Business Networking Ltd 2021. All rights reserved.

There's lots of networking advice, which asks us to consider whether conversational groups are "open" (available to approach) or "closed" (difficult to approach and break into).

The advice might be "Don't approach Group 1 (closed) but go ahead with Group 3 (open)."

Even if we don't consider ourselves skilled social observers, it is fairly easy for us to spot when people are engrossed in an animated conversation or perhaps are old friends who want to catch up personally, to the temporary exclusion of others. Group 2 might be an example of this.

Social science would again suggest that context is all important. Some very formal events (black tie perhaps) might set a social code where we certainly would not impose ourselves on Group 1. Or at least not until it looked like it was fragmenting, or it was obvious the conversation has reached a hiatus.

Alternatively, there are other more relaxed social contexts (an office BBQ?) where it would be perfectly acceptable to "break in" to Group 1.

The other key factor is politeness. It may seem obvious but cutting in and overpowering a conversation will not win many supporters. A simple 'May I join you?' is enough to persuade most groups that we are worthy of being allowed in.

It's also worth mentioning the advice of Professor Dunbar, who states:

"The upper limit on the number of people who can maintain a functional conversation is just four; add an extra person and I can guarantee that within 30 seconds, it will be two separate conversations."

So, we may need to bear in mind that a group of six people is not a conversation between six, but most likely two (or more?) separate conversations.

Approaching conversational groups is really a matter of being polite and relying on our judgment of the situation. There's no guarantee that Group 3 will be easier to approach than Group 4 (or vice versa). It depends.

The Restorative Niche

This term is a favorite of Professor Brian Little of the University of Cambridge. An expert in personality, his TED Talk is highly recommended.

Professor Little's coining of the phrase refers to the practice of finding a haven of quiet and solitude to recharge our batteries.

In a networking context, it could mean taking a quick five-minute time out. This provides an opportunity to assess results so far and think about the achievement of our networking goals, flexing or revising our plans as necessary.

Again, this plays to personality traits of extraversion and introversion. The biological theory for these types of behavior (see Eysenck 1947) rests upon stimulus of the brain.

As Eysenckian theory goes, the brains of extraverts are understimulated. They, therefore, take up opportunities to seek out stimulation to restore an equilibrium. This may account for extreme extrovert behavior that is often described as thrill-seeking.

Conversely, according to theory, the brains of introverts are overstimulated. This means they seek out opportunities to dampen down this over stimulus.

Introverted behavior might then be evidenced by removal from the situation, such as someone seeking refuge in a good book. But this wouldn't do at a normal networking event!

Professor Little's own recommendation? This involves finding the monastic sanctuary of a WC cubicle!

Stay Late (The Stay Late Play)

Accepting constraints of time and energy, staying until the end of an event can pay dividends.

Remembering "primacy and recency" and good early impressions, we have an equally good opportunity to make a lasting impression as the event draws to a close.

It's often said that some of the best conversations strike up as people are leaving. At this point, we'll find that groups have formed where people feel comfortable with each other.

This informality spills over into freedom of speech and more relaxed conversation. Our messages around who we are and what we do start to sink in.

In this fertile ground, people have more time to think about the implications of what they are hearing. When social barriers are lowered in this way, opportunities often appear.

So, notwithstanding the restrictions of the next meeting in the daily diary or the final train home, we should consider staying as long as we can.

But ... (The Don't Stay Too Late Play)

There's a slight risk in staying on late at an event.

We might stop the organizers from being free to have their preagreed postevent debrief. They don't want to discuss such things within our earshot. Also, they won't thank us for getting in their way and preventing them from returning home to friends and family.

The solution? If we do decide to stay on (and this is a judgment call like any other), let's keep our eyes and ears open.

If we should feel that we are overstaying our welcome, let's just say our thankyous and goodbyes as quickly as possible and then exit.

With any luck, the event organizers will realize what a savvy, self-knowledgeable lot we are. Who knows, we may even get a special invite to their next event?

Strategic Business Networking - further explained:

In 2015, a *Harvard Business Review* article was published with the heading "99% of Networking Is a Waste of Time." This slightly provocative headline led to many other news media commentaries following like a comet trail in its wake.

During his visit to the World Economic Forum in Davos, Switzerland, networking supremo Rich Stromback (known as "Mr. Davos") remarked that our labored attempts to connect with our fellow men and women at countless venues and events throughout the land are, mostly, all for naught.

But what Rich Stromback said deserves closer analysis.

In fact, while he recognized the value of high-profile Davos-type events, because they offer unrivaled opportunity for face-to-face contact with key people, Stromback's perceptive observation was that "99 percent of Davos is information or experience you can get elsewhere, on your own time-frame and in a more comfortable manner."

But the killer comment is Stromback's response to a question on whether networking represents "real work." His answer was most certainly, but *"you need to be extremely efficient and focus on what is truly essential."*

So, how can we increase our networking efficiency and focus?

Today's time-poor work/life environment requires us to adopt a new approach to our networking practice. If we ignore this, we can spend valuable time attending events and building networks that don't deliver on our needs. In effect, we'll end up doing the right things, but in the wrong way.

Most basic networking falls under the definitions of "operational" (relationships required to get the job done) and "personal" (via membership of groups or, e.g., to provide a source of coaching or mentoring).

The key however is Strategic Business Networking. Only this plugs the networker into the collaborative power to achieve both individual and organizational goals.

Herminia Ibarra, Charles Handy professor of Organisational Behaviour at the London Business School, England defines strategic networking as " ... the ability to marshal information, support, and resources from one sector of a network to achieve results in another."

As we have said before, your start point should therefore be to decide what, exactly, you want from your networking. How much resource, including time commitment, do you have available to devote to it? What tangible outcomes are you seeking (or being told) to achieve?

We should always question whether our normal default mode of connecting with people is serving us in the best way possible. And, if necessary, think again.

Take Action

- Consider how conversational groups are oriented, but context will always be important.
- Politeness always pays.
- Take a timeout, if needed.
- Staying late offers opportunities. But also, possibly, some risks.

CHAPTER 8

Building Mentor and Advocate Networks (The Mentor Play)

Mentors and Advocates

We made the point earlier in the book that none of us can do it all alone. All successful people rely on a network of trusted advisers. People who can help us to develop. People who can talk things through. People who themselves can introduce us to others may also have a valuable perspective.

We don't need to get into the differences between mentors and advocates. Suffice to say, we are referring to those who can be generally helpful in our mission to develop our careers or professional presence.

Mentors buy into our personal project. They understand what we as the mentee (the individual being mentored) is seeking to achieve. They are on the lookout for opportunities to add to the mix.

And the best mentor relationships stand the test of time. They grow as we grow.

Building Relationships

In many ways, building a relationship with mentors is no different to building relationships with other people.

And we are referring to mentors in the plural. There's no rule that says we should only have one person as a mentor. It's a sensible strategy to have a range of expertise to call upon. Two heads (or more!) are better than one.

Dr. Heidi Grant's excellent book "No One Understands You: and What to Do About It," talks of three lenses through which we all might be perceived. The Trust Lens, The Power Lens, and The Ego Lens.

Of particular interest is The Power Lens because this is often the relationship that is perceived by the mentee or mentor, or both. The mentee might see the mentor as relatively more powerful (and the mentor may feel the same way).

Some might say this imbalance is implicit within the mentee/mentor "power relationship."

The flip side is this relative power might distort how we, as prospective mentees, are seen. Dr. Grant makes the point that "Power causes perceivers to rely more heavily on stereotypes and prior expectations. This makes it more difficult for you to distinguish yourself as a unique individual in their eyes."

If developing a relationship with a mentor now sounds like a tough task, help is at hand.

It comes in the form of "instrumentality."

Instrumentality suggests that people behave or act in a certain way because they are motivated to select that behavior over other options. This is due to what they expect the result of that behavior to be.

High achievers, such as mentors, tend to display this instrumentality focus. They keep busy with their goals, possibly to the exclusion of others who they perceive as less powerful.

But if we can become someone who helps that powerful person to achieve their goals, to facilitate instrumentality, we can bring ourselves to their attention. The mentor can suddenly realize our potential.

In doing so, they will find the time and energy to perceive us as we really are. We can then take the opportunity to engage them in our personal project.

A natural by-product of this is the power relationship changes. And we can justifiably argue that it changes in a way to fuel the attainment of respective (and mutual) goals. Both mentee and mentor are spurred on to achieve more.

Asking for Help?

It can be a tricky thing: asking for help with our job search, client building challenge, or career development problem.

So, why do it? As in "Ask for help?"

We don't always need to disclose vulnerabilities. Furthermore, no friend, contact, or mentor wants to feel pressured into "helping" when they really can't, or don't have the time.

A better approach is that proposed by informational discussion. Here we are not asking for help, but simply seeking advice, information, or guidance.

Research shows that advice seeking can be very powerful in terms of building relationships with prospective mentors or advocates.

This points to four main effects:

1. Learning. Information is useful. That throwaway comment about a contact or prospective employer can turn out to be a nugget of gold.
2. Perspective taking. Our contact can be brought into our worldview and, similarly, we can better understand theirs.
3. Flattery. Asking someone for advice elevates that person and grants them prestige. Who doesn't warm to being seen in this way?
4. Commitment. Now we're getting somewhere! If the method of asking is sufficiently skillful and the contact sufficiently amenable and well-connected, we can move the relationship to a position of advocacy. Very soon we have someone batting on our side, taking our corner and operating on our behalf.

But we should exercise care! All the previous points, and particularly number four, need to be done in a genuine, open, and honest manner.

Anything short of this might lead people to feel manipulated.

The Right Way

It can be difficult to judge the correct approach with mentors. We sometimes agonize over whether we've got it right.

But there's a simple way for us to get into the heads of mentors to really understand them better.

And that's to become a mentor ourselves.

It's very easy these days to find opportunities to mentor others. The education sector, professional bodies, and social enterprise groups are just some examples.

Many organizations formalize the rules by which their mentors work and insist that a process of "contracting" is carried out. Both the mentor and the mentee therefore understand things such as time commitment, confidentiality, and at what point the mentoring will conclude.

This way it's easy to give mentoring a shot, without entering a time-consuming or long-term obligation and mentors invariably find the experience rewarding and enriching.

But I Don't Want to Brag ...

Setting out our case in the presence of a prospective mentor often involves talking about our achievements.

However, for most of us, blowing our own trumpet is hard to do. Why? Well, from a very young age we may have been told: "Don't boast, don't show off, don't stick your head above the parapet." After all, nobody likes a Smart Alec.

However, we can all think of people who seem to have the uncanny knack of spelling out their successes at the right time, in the right place, in the right way, and to the people who matter. And they seem to be able to do this without an ounce of shame or self-criticism.

So, what's going on? When does authentic self-projection spill over into bragging and hubris?

In all societies, there are rules or cultural norms that govern modesty. Similarly, there are situations where boastful behavior is tolerated without the individual being labeled a braggart.

So how we can successfully "Blag that brag?" In other words, how we can sing our own praises—even when we don't really wish to?

One technique is to make our bragging relevant to the situation. For example, if we are asked to extol our virtues during a job interview, the path is clear for us to do just that. It's acceptable within the context.

Likewise, if someone else should initiate the subject of the brag, we can join in with our own story. If anyone suffers the disdain of others, it will be the initiator and not us.

Context also plays a part in the conditions applying to the listener at the time. If they are attempting to multitask, their attention can be divided or under pressure.

Think of recruitment processes that involve group interaction among the job candidates. Recruiters who moderate the group discussion assignments are often multitasking. Here, the positive information underlying the boast can be absorbed without attributing poor manners to the person who made it.

It also seems to matter in the sense of making comparisons. Telling others that we are better than them (or another) will make us look like someone who has a sense of superiority and who enjoys putting people down.

Alternatively, talking about our own self-improvement and making a comparison of how we were then and how much better we are now, offers a much more balanced perspective.

There's a bonus if we can tie this into the self-knowledge required to recognize our own development areas and the effort made to improve. So, we could say, "Since realizing x, I've worked hard to improve my ... ."

Mixing a boast with flattery sometimes helps. In a job interview situation, it shows we've done our homework on the organization, while also suggesting a good fit between our values and theirs. For example, "I share the company's award-winning interest in environmental protection; in my last role, I was responsible for reducing waste by x percent."

If we have done our homework on the mentor's achievements and we genuinely have a shared interest or achievement, the same approach would work in a mentor situation.

Social proof can come to the aid of bragging: people are persuaded by the actions of others. Another strategy can be to have someone else, a friend or ally, speak for us.

While a reciprocal agreement ("You brag for me, and I'll brag for you") might come across as false, this relatively risk-free way does confirm the importance of developing supportive relationships both in our workplace and more widely in our professions.

People who are prepared to speak up for us, either as advocates or mentors, can have a very powerful effect on how we are seen and perceived. This might just be the difference between our being offered that golden opportunity, or watching it pass by.

A recent phenomenon is the "humblebrag." This is said to have originated from the sentence limiting idiosyncrasies of social media, such as Twitter.

It's a kind of "get in, get out quick" strategy in which the brag is presented in the form of, or coupled with, a complaint. One facet is intended to be tempered by the other, for example, "Since my Harvard Business Review article went viral, I've been absolutely snowed-under with e-mails!"

As attractive as it might seem, recent research suggests the humblebrag doesn't work. Furthermore, it has revealed that it would be better just to complain or, if bragging is a must, then deliver the boast as honestly as we feel we can.

The latter technique is more important than it first looks. There are social costs associated with being direct. For example, others may perceive us as insensitive.

Taking the alternative extreme, a Uriah Heep "ever so humble" approach to extolling our virtues can also have a social cost. False modesty is disapproved of as much as humblebragging; the teller might be perceived as both obnoxious and insincere.

Is bragging worth it? As with most things social, we need to think about the context.

We might also think about mixing a subtle social cocktail. In this way, the brag is blended with other ingredients, while avoiding the brash humblebrag.

In other words, a cocktail that's more Mai Tai than Snakebite!

Raising Our Head Above the Parapet

At the start of the book, we mentioned how competitive the world of work and commerce can be.

Given that we can't work against this situation, let's see how we may be able to work with it to raise our profile with prospective mentors.

Networking events that feature speakers as a focus can be useful for building relationships with possible mentors. So, we may be thinking of a situation where there is a single speaker giving a presentation on a topic of interest to them, or maybe a panel of speakers moderated by a host who keeps the discussion on track.

Both types of event and others benefit from a feature that is particularly valuable to us as prospective mentees. This is the Question and Answer slot.

Event Questioning (The Q and A Play)

The Q and A is often used by event promoters to give attendees an opportunity to speak directly with the expert. It stands to reason that it can be a useful way to start a mentoring relationship if we happen to be one of the people asking a question.

The first tip is to make sure that we have researched beforehand so that our question demonstrates prior knowledge of the topic and some understanding of the perspective taken by the speaker. The question should also be short and to the point. As we will be speaking in a room full of people, it's worth rehearsing the wording to make sure we present ourselves effectively.

The second is to position our question to take advantage of primacy and recency effects. That is, we want to be the first person to ask a question or the last.

Given the unknowns around timing for the Q and A and how it might be moderated, it's far easier to opt for being the first questioner. We just need to make sure that, as the floor is opened, we are in the eye line of the moderator and quick off the mark in raising a hand.

If a microphone is being circulated, we need to wait calmly for this to arrive. If we blurt out our question immediately, there's a risk it may not be heard by the panel or speaker (or indeed, appear on a recording of the event if there is one).

Microphone in hand, we can then pause momentarily. Not too long to imply that we have forgotten our question (!), but long enough to build some anticipation around what will be said. It's also surprising how often a slight imposed pause within the room can have the effect of establishing authority on the part of the questioner.

Once the question has been asked, we should make a point of listening patiently to the answer and taking a mental note of any snippets that might be significant for subsequent relationship building.

It's enough to leave the questioning at this point and not to ask a follow up (unless we are encouraged to do so by the speaker or moderator). We should let other people in the room have their say.

As a Q and A generally happens at the close of a speaker slot or panel discussion, it usually ends as some other part of the evening commences, for example, break out for drink and food.

It's at this point, as the Q and A breaks up, that we should make our move.

Without appearing overeager, we can approach the speaker on a one-to-one basis and pick up on the questioning theme. We then have an opportunity to weave in our prepared messages around who we are, what we do, and our personal career project.

It's a fact that event speakers tend to hold a focus for all those attending an event (this is one of the reasons why professional specialists develop speaking topics and speaking skills—they are used as a marketing tool).

This means that we may find ourselves in a queue to get in front of that person. But the groundwork will have been done through our carefully posed question. If this part has gone well, when we appear before them we will gain recognition from the speaker.

This has a curious but valuable effect based on that remembrance: First, it elevates our status relative to others in the room. Secondly, it smooths the path to valuable engagement with them as we move seamlessly into our networking dialogue and key messages.

The Benjamin Franklin Effect (The BF Play)

A second technique for raising our profile owes its name to one of the Founding Fathers of the United States. Benjamin Franklin (1706–1790) was a renowned author, printer, political theorist, politician, scientist, inventor, civic activist, statesman, and diplomat.

Franklin was also a people person and master networker.

In his long and varied political life, he encountered many situations where he needed to build relationships with those who were more foe than friend.

In his autobiography, Franklin tells how he turned around the animosity of a rival politician into friendship:

Having heard that he had in his library a certain very scarce and curious book, I wrote a note to him, expressing my desire of perusing that book and requesting he would do me the favor of lending it to me for a few days. He sent it immediately, and I return'd it in about a week with another note, expressing strongly my sense of the favor. When we next met in the House, he spoke to me (which he had never done before), and with great civility; and he ever after manifested a readiness to serve me on all occasions, so that we became great friends ...

Now, we're familiar with the concept of reciprocity: you do something for me and I'll do something for you. And the "doing" here is something of obvious value at a time when books were scarce and therefore highly desirable possessions.

So, we might be thinking that Franklin offered his political foe a favor to build the relationship in expectation of gaining something in return?

But Franklin didn't lend a book, he asked to borrow one ...

The "Benjamin Franklin Effect" is considered an example of cognitive dissonance. This describes a situation where there is an obvious mismatch (or dissonance) between an individual's thoughts and attitudes, and their behavior.

The rival politician should not have been willing to lend the book to Franklin, given his animosity toward Franklin's political views. But he did.

Franklin cleverly focused on common ground—a shared love of books—to engage a psychological principle: if someone helps you, they'll be ready to help you again.

And more so, than if you have helped them and you are just expecting a favor in return.

The eagle-eyed reader will notice that we've slipped into using the word "help." But its use is appropriate here.

Our lesson is to make it easy for someone to help us out because this is a great relationship-building tool (but notice also that Franklin didn't explicitly ask for help, he just asked to borrow a book!).

Asking a question within a Q and A context and engaging the Benjamin Franklin Effect are both powerful strategies to raise our profiles with prospective mentors.

Mentors—A Final Word (The "Just Move on" Play)

It can sometimes be a real kick in the teeth when we approach a prospective mentor. And then ... we hear nothing further. Diddly squat.

As tough to take as this might seem, and tough because we've prob-ably invested a lot of ourselves in making the approach in the first place, there's a golden rule to follow.

This is: Pick yourself up, dust yourself down … and start all over again.

Mentors don't have to respond. It's up to them. In the same way that we are trying to pick winners among the people we approach, they are perfectly entitled to do the same. They are wrong to ignore us of course, but that's their prerogative. Move on.

Never Give Up

Every wannabee first-time author has a story about how tough it was to get published. Famously, J. K. Rowling was turned down 12 times by publishers. Believe me, I have my own!

Part of the problem is that publishing has, in my opinion, become very much like other forms of media such as film or music. In these spheres and others, it's now very difficult to break through without some form of top-level help and funding. And even Simon Cowell, the creator of the globally successful "X Factor" and "Got Talent" fran-chises, doesn't have enough money to help everyone.

Back in my heyday, the 1970s, new music artistes were regularly given multimillion-dollar contracts for a first or subsequent album. The champagne, and other substances, flowed!

Publishing business models now run on very tight margins. The disruption caused by Internet giants such as Amazon has caused a tsu-nami of job losses and slashing of profits for those still in the game.

Some publishers tried to pivot to offer an Amazon-light model, others are still clinging on to old ways. Maybe the owners hope they can hang on and get a soft landing to their own retirement. Should they try to sell up, I doubt they'd realize much in value; the world has changed and the good old days of bumper profits and long, lingering client lunches are over.

Many criticize Amazon and their kin. I don't.

Surely there's a case for saying that the gravy train of the old ways rolled on for just a little bit too long. Did it really promote the brightest and the best? Look at how the music industry has morphed from a hits chart where the same old names would appear regularly, to one where we have a huge number of new and exciting acts and the chance to experience contemporary music from many, many genres.

This is good. It expands our horizons and makes us better people. My own experience is one of pivoting from playing the same old tracks to one where I now love to listen to many kinds of music, including the latest offerings from Jonas Blue, Kim Petras, and HAIM (ignore these names if you are reading this some years after publication of this book. You won't know all of them!).

I'm not taking anything away from those established artistes who continually reinvent themselves. David Bowie was an absolute paragon in this respect.

But there are many others, including one of my favorites, Alice Cooper. Alice (real name Vince Furnier, of course) has been through many travails, including being close to death on more than one occasion—the result of battles with alcohol addiction.

But I think it might be hard to find many with as much talent and, most importantly, such humility and humanity, who go about their life giving generously to others. And without making a song and dance about it (little is known about his Arizona Teen Center charity, open to all teens 12–20 years old, and providing free access to musical instruments, music lessons, song writing, and coaching).

So, if this "New England" opens up wider opportunities for all, then I think it is a very good thing. As is anything that levels up the world and challenges society's many baked-in privileges.

What does this mean for networking?

Well, number one is: Don't be dissuaded by anything you feel sets you at a disadvantage. Having this in your head isn't helpful to my cause or yours. Push through any negative thoughts and get on with it.

Number two is much less wordy: Never give up.

Paul Simon's most successful studio album, released in 1986, is *Graceland*. But the story of the album, how it came to be made and what preceded it, is a fascinating one.

By the 1980s, Simon's success of the 1970s (q.v. *Bridge Over Troubled Water*) had faded. His relationship with his musical partner, Art Garfunkel, always built on a degree of artistic struggle, had pretty much run its course. His marriage to Carrie Fisher, the actor, was over and Simon himself went through a period of poor mental health.

But *Graceland* proved to be a turning point that moved Simon on to even greater heights. The album is estimated to have sold over 16 million copies worldwide.

One of my favorite songs on the album is the lead single "You Can Call Me Al." Funnily enough, it was also one of my dad's favorites too. A humorous man, he enjoyed the playful lines and couplets of the lyrics.

The title is said to have come to Simon after he and his first wife, Peggy, were invited to a New York party hosted by the eminent conductor and composer, Pierre Boulez.

The famous man met them at the apartment door to welcome them in. But having no clue who they were, despite the invitation, he announced them to the other guests as "Al and Betty!"

Referring to this in a song makes me think that Simon is attempting to pop the balloon of pomposity. Perhaps he and his wife were invited to the occasion as token guests, with no real thought of who they were or what their interests might have been. This reminds me of social gatherings where the magpie host just wants an opportunity to brag about who attended what and when. Some networking events have the same inauthentic flavor.

But there's another clever lyric that also speaks to me:

"I want a shot at redemption" (© Paul Simon 1986. All rights reserved).

This is an interesting line. What does it mean? Well, I had to turn to the dictionary to discover:

"To have the chance, the opportunity, to make things right so that others will see that your motivations, your intentions are in good faith and for everyone's benefit."

That's good enough for me.

Contradictions: It's funny how life can be full of contradictions.

- I've given a rather poor account of Pierre Boulez. By his own admission he was a man with several character flaws, including being described by many as a bully. But Boulez was also someone who could show momentous compassion for others. When a long-term mentor was paralyzed by a stroke and unable to work, he is reported to have sent scripts to national radio in that person's name, thereby allowing them to collect much-needed royalty fees.
- *Graceland* sounds like an instant and gargantuan success, doesn't it? It wasn't. It struggled to reach the heights of the 1987 UK album charts and spent only one week in the Top 100, ranked at a lowly 98th position. In the United States, it fared slightly better, helped by spending over 97 weeks in the charts. The Grammy Awards of 1987 provided a boost that we might recognize as a broadcast (i.e., one to many), rather than any kind of viral, person-to-person spread. But there were signs of it garnering support informally via "social proof" (people are persuaded by the actions of others). On the face of it, the album is a typical example of an "overnight success" that was in fact a very slow burn.

Remember. Never give up.

Take Action

- Start building a mentor network today. And become a mentor yourself.
- Consider how you can engage when mentors display instrumentality.
- Use informational discussion. Seek information, advice, and guidance before using the word help.
- Beware of bragging anywhere other than the right place and time.

- Be strategic in building your mentor network. Use the opportunities presented by event Q and A sessions (The Q and A Play) and the Benjamin Franklin Effect (The BF Play).
- When prospective mentors don't respond, it's not that they won't help you. It's that they perhaps can't. Move on.
- Never give up.

CHAPTER 9

Social Media and Networking (The Know Your Audience Play)

Social media has a fantastic place within networking and offers many opportunities.

But it might be a mistake in a book such as this to talk about specific features and advantages. The pace of change within social media is so great, things will have moved on even before the ink has dried on this draft script!

Rather, it might be better to concentrate on where and where not to employ what social media offers us.

It's a Great Way to Network

Um, no it isn't; if, by the strict definition of what we are about, personal relationships are the objective.

The value of our networks and our value to our network partners cannot be measured by the number of LinkedIn Connections, Twitter followers, or Facebook "Likes." It's more to do with depth and integrity of the connection.

There's an old joke about a salesperson and their sales manager. They are discussing the former's annual performance review. "What do you want me to get?" asks the salesperson, "Quality of sales lead, or quantity?"

"It's not a question of one or the other, I want *both*!" replied the sales manager.

And as it is with networking. We need to think of mixed-method strategies.

Social media offers unprecedented opportunities on two fronts. First, it allows us to expand our networks within, across, and beyond our normal parameters.

Sending a LinkedIn connection request to someone across the globe is easy to do. This is "weak ties" in action. And remember that weak ties are "indispensable to individuals' opportunities."

Secondly, although it won't replace normal face-to-face contact, social media is an extremely valuable tool to build a bridge with prospective contacts, mentors, and advocates.

This bridge building can be done through "connecting," "follows," "likes," "comments," "mentions," and all the other social media engagement actions.

From this bridgehead, the relationship can be developed into the more traditional forms of contact, whether by e-mail, telephone, video call, or, ultimately, face to face. We can see this as a series of stepping stones.

Thinking that social media can do it all, and even replace the need for personal direct contact, might be misguided.

On the other hand, valuable weak tie connections can remain current through the judicious use of social media features that allow us to stay in touch by commenting on job moves, anniversaries, birthdays, and so on.

I Can Tell Everyone My News

Social media can be a great self-projection platform. For example, our LinkedIn profiles are a very convenient repository of who we are, what we do, and the value we can bring.

But there is a dark side, because there's a danger in how we present our profile, as well as in how we interact with the platform.

One aspect of social media is immediacy. This can sometimes lead to inadvisable "off the cuff" comments which, with the benefit of hindsight, might have been more guarded. The developers of social media are very skilled in human psychology. They know how to "press our buttons" and have us do things which, in normal circumstances and with careful thought, we wouldn't do.

We should also recognize the very real constraints upon those of us who are employees, where a breach of corporate compliance policies can lead to very severe sanction.

It can help to bear in mind a simple guideline. The best form of networking is not about incessantly tooting our own horn, but lifting others up through positivity and encouragement.

In these respects, it's a little bit like the golden rules for improv theater:

- You don't have to be funny.
- Don't deny (i.e., go with the flow).
- You can look good if you make your partner look good.

We should structure our social media interactions accordingly. Sharing is caring. And, if in doubt, leave it out.

The Medium Is the Message (McLuhan 1964)

It's important not to waste time on platforms that don't conform to our core values and messages or, indeed, those of our target network. We might love LinkedIn, but our desired contact may be an avid Tweeter. There isn't an immediate match of platforms.

For example, in occupations such as journalism, media, and learning and development, the most popular tool is Twitter. So, if we're looking to contact a journalist or someone who operates within the host of industries classified as "creative" (publishing, books, film, etc.), this ought to be the preferred medium.

And here the immediacy of Twitter can be considered a strength, rather than a weakness. There are many colloquial stories of how contacts have been made this way and jobs, business, and clients have been won as a result.

Filling the Unforgiving Minute (The Kipling Play)

Kipling's verse, "If," contains the words:
"If you can fill the unforgiving minute
With sixty seconds' worth of distance run,
Yours is the Earth and everything that's in it ... "
　　　　　—Rudyard Kipling, "Rewards and Fairies" 1909

It's a kind of plea to seize the day and make the most of the time available to all of us, right down to the "unforgiving minute."

And there's the rub with social media. It is, by definition, somewhat addictive.

This is no accident. Social media platforms together employ an army of social scientists and behavioral experts who know very well how to keep us users tapping away. And before we know it, the day has passed by.

Extreme levels of social media addiction are now recognized as a pathology by mental health professionals, as are the symptoms of "social media burnout."

So, the approach recommended by Strategic Business Networking is to have a balanced networking method. And, rather like the strong tie/weak tie, exclusive network/inclusive network mix, we should ensure that our networking practice benefits from a balance of both online and face-to-face activity.

Catch 22 (The Power Play)

To demonstrate where social media can be very powerful, here's a story in the context of career development. It may be a few years old, but it's still highly relevant.

Leigh, a young customer service professional, was looking to develop his career. Unfortunately, Leigh was coming up against a common problem: the "Catch 22" situation, where he needed a job to get experience but needed experience to get a job!

Within LinkedIn, Leigh was a member of a professional group. It occurred to him to reach out to other members for guidance.

Joining a LinkedIn group can be a fantastic stepping stone to get to where we want to go.

Leigh's opening wording is a great example of how to phrase a request:

Customer Service Support Manager
DDNS CONSULTING LTD · Part-time
Jan 2017 – Present · 4 yrs 4 mos
London Area, United Kingdom

Experience
Hi everyone. I'm due to finish my part-time MSc studies shortly. I have been job hunting and researching junior psychologist roles. In my present and past duties, I have been handling client enquiries and serving customer needs on a regular basis. I get great feedback! But I notice that most positions require me to have at least 12 months' pure psychology experience.

So the question for me is, how do I gain this experience? I want to start my career, but feel that I'm on the back foot from the get-go! I'd really love to hear if anyone has any thoughts on how to gain relevant experience? I've followed up on voluntary/social enterprise work, but the only thing I can find is Call Centre work, the kind of thing I'm already doing.

The request is friendly, personalized, and gets to the point quickly. It also states Leigh's issue in a human way—he hasn't given up, but we can sense his frustration.

This powerful messaging clearly struck a chord from the many responses Leigh received. Here's a quick selection from around 19 individual responses containing information, advice, and support:

Hi Leigh. Would you have time to volunteer for another charity closely allied to your objective? It's amazing some of the opps that can come out of this work! Or find a great recruiter who can 'sell' your transferable skills to an employer? Org Psych/HR is difficult to get into, no idea why but I love it! Good luck and reach out if you need support!

Hi. Here's a good tip. LinkedIn regularly offer their Premium service free for 30 days. You can always unsubscribe! Select the recruiter option and this can give you access to a lot of useful tools that might help! Just a thought! Wishing you a successful job search! ☺

Good on you, Leigh! It can indeed be a challenge to get into I/O Psych when the majority of roles require you to have experience. Unpaid internships are not always the answer either.
I've known several people who have approached companies directly. You just need to come up with a compelling idea on how you can help them. Maybe something from your Customer Service experience? You must have lots of stories! Perhaps you could shadow someone in HR/Org Design at your current employer? Find the roles that don't actually say 'psychologist', but still act as a stepping stone to where you want to be...
As a final tip, why not register with agencies who specialise in temporary work? Companies often use these to manage workflows when it gets busy. This might get you a foot in the door. The rest is up to you! Wishing you every success!

We can see there's an awful lot of goodwill out there, just waiting to be tapped into. It's always a life-affirming experience to see others providing guidance in such a selfless way.

But what Leigh does next is equally valuable. He takes the time to say thank you.

Leigh Sullivan **Author**   1s ···
Customer Service Support Manager

Thank you everyone. I really do appreciate all the ideas and also the
kind support and encouragement! 😊

Leigh is currently pursuing his dream of a professional career, having
found employment based on the advice he received. Good luck to him!

The strategies outlined previously can apply to all social media. But, as
Friends Reunited, Vine, and Google+ demonstrate, platforms can come
and go.

So, let's confine ourselves to one of the biggest, LinkedIn.

LinkedIn (The LinkedIn Play)

LinkedIn is a great tool for helping to build networks. But it's not a complete substitute for all the other types of networking activity: coffee chats,
drinks at the bar, lunches, evening events, use of other social media, and
so forth.

The problem with writing about LinkedIn is that it is, necessarily,
a dynamic platform. Things change all the time. And that's right and
proper.

But it means that, as soon as the ink dries on this page, whatever is
said will be out of date.

Ok, having got that off our chest shall we proceed?

This section will cover three things about LinkedIn and explore some
techniques that will help with our networking. The good news is that
these techniques contain principles that are universal.

This means that, first, they are unlikely to be affected by the latest
version of LinkedIn. And secondly, we'll be able to apply them in other
contexts. Sounds pretty good doesn't it?

The three areas are:

- Populating your LinkedIn profile.
- Asking people for LinkedIn recommendations.
- 'Network effects.'

Populating Your LinkedIn Profile (The Profile Play)

The profile photo is very important, if not vital. We are visual beings.

Because we talk of the five senses; touch, smell, hearing, taste, and sight, it often seems that sight is lumped in with the other four.

But we could draw a special distinction with sight. The organs we use to see are not "connected" to the brain. To a large extent, they *are* the brain. And this makes sense from an evolutionary standpoint, recognizing just how important the sense of sight would be to our first ancestors.

So, sight is important. But so are faces.

As humans our brains are attuned to searching for and recognizing faces (another evolutionary idea, we need to be able to recognize both friends and foe. Anthropologists refer to this kind of thing as "adaptive"; being able to see confers an evolutionary advantage).

Reputable and replicable scientific studies have shown that even very young babies can recognize faces, particularly those of their parents. If we might be skeptical of this, we just need to think about how a baby, only a few days' old, will smile in recognition when it sees its mother.

Still skeptical? We can try it with any nearby baby of our acquaintance!

And being attuned to faces is the very reason why we sometimes see face profiles when we look up at clouds in the sky, or why people often "see" Christ's image on a slice of toast.

So, first thing, we need to make sure that our LinkedIn profile has a photo that we are happy with.

One good tip here, as well as getting technical things such as lighting and so on right, is that the photo needs to depict where we are headed. Not where we have been.

The prom photo, beer in hand, looks lovely. But if we are aspiring to become the world's youngest University professor, or Chair of the Federal Reserve, then a more appropriate image is called for.

Now the "About" section.

This needs to be written in the first party for example, "I am a brilliant psychologist …" or "I want to be the next Chair of the Federal Reserve." Not like a CV which, in the United Kingdom at least, tends to be written in the third party.

The "About" section needs to be a mix of qual and quant. That is, text, plus some metrics. This way we catch all the fishes who read it, not just one type. We are not just a "one-club golfer."

For example, *"I am an accomplished salesperson. In my first season, I was responsible for direct sales of USD XX. I then built on this to my best season to achieve USD YY."*

We should aim for the right mix of humility and self-projection. But never, ever lie (as if we would!).

Asking People for LinkedIn Recommendations (The Recommendations Play)

Recommendations matter. "People are persuaded by the actions of others" is a saying that has been shown to be correct in very many psychological experiments. If someone who knows us says we are good, then other people whether they know us or not will tend to believe this.

So, we need to get some. Maybe five or so max (although some people go for gold and have hundreds of the darn things!).

Here's a four-step method that works:

Step 1: Don't ask for any old recommendation. Ask for the recommendation we want! No one benefits from a duff recommendation or, even worse, one that sounds like all the others.

BUT people are busy (well, good people are anyway). They don't always have time to think things through in the way we want them to. Or they may not even *want* to give us a recommendation!

Step 2: So, we need to ask for the recommendation we want. And in the *right way*.

But, do it in a way that (a) doesn't pressurize them and (b) allows them an exit strategy if they can't or won't provide it now. This way, we don't damage the relationship. After all, they are not saying "no," they are just saying "no, not now."

Step 3: So, how to make the ask? LinkedIn will walk us through the process. In fact, the developers have made a cracking job of this at present. It is very easy to do, as we just need to populate a field with some text. Here's what we can do:

Paragraph one gets the recommender's attention. This could be something about say, a memory jogger of working together, or maybe that special project when we were with them for a few months. Or perhaps we're asking a family member who knows us well enough. In which case, a simple "Hi" will do.

Paragraph(s) two (and beyond) ask the specific questions. We can call this "the meat in the sandwich." Some examples are shown as follows.

The ending paragraph says something like "No problem if you are not able to do this now ... I will still buy you a coffee when we next meet ... I still love you ..." (no, don't take that literally!). Just give the recommender space to exit for now if they need to. No hard feelings.

Step 4: Finally, we'll diarize clearly so that we can check what we get back in return, or even if we get nothing back (a bad sign, possibly?). Never push for a recommendation. Take it steady. According to the UK Highway Code, a green light at a traffic junction doesn't mean "go." It means "Proceed with caution!"

If it feels like we are pushing against a closed door, we should back off. And gracefully.

The Meat in the Sandwich (The Meat Play)

Here's how this can be tackled:

Can I ask a quick question?

If you were speaking to another person about me, what would you say in the following areas?

- How *quickly* do I make things happen. Am I an "on it" person?
- I'm particularly interested in comments around *my XXXXX skills.*
- *How* do I work? (Do I make things easy for you? Am I pleasant to deal with? Are my interventions timely?)
- Also *what* do I do differently that's particularly effective (and others don't do)?

Alert: For all these text comment examples, it would be best for us to think a little and use our own words. Whenever we try to parrot the words of another, or just simply copy and paste, we fail to come across as an authentic person. Result? We won't get the recommendation we want. Let's play with it a bit. Who knows, we might be able to come up with something even better? Remember "Proceed with caution."

'Network Effects'

To use LinkedIn effectively and to harness its undoubted power to the full, we need to achieve 'network effects'.

The standard definition of network effects is that they exist when a product or service's value to users increases as the number of users grow. Put in terms of our own LinkedIn network, the more connections we have (and, of course, the more we engage with them), the more valuable our network of connections will become to us. A good start point is 500 connections.

So, the take home point is that we shouldn't paddle around in the village pond. We need to get out there on the ocean where the big fish are and grow our network. And there's a very easy way to start doing this by importing contacts in bulk from our existing address book databases and connecting with them. LinkedIn has a great search function which explains how to do this.

Computational Social Science and Why Microsoft Paid US$26.2bn for LinkedIn

Why is social media awash with content from marketers who promise the earth and who claim they can help us "game" the LinkedIn system?

From New York to the Netherlands, they reckon to understand what drives the behemoth; in particular, all the rules and processes (the underlying algorithm):

How the LinkedIn Algorithm Works and How to Make it Work for You (Hootsuite)

Beginner's Guide on How to Beat the LinkedIn Algorithm (Social Champ)

And even Forbes gets in on the act:

5 Tips to Game the LinkedIn Algorithm

I disagree. And I don't think it's that simple. But LinkedIn's masters probably don't mind the chatter and publicity!

What makes me think this way? Put simply, why in 2016 would Microsoft pay US$26.2bn for something that was easy to "game?" After all, the algorithm and systems data is principally what this payment covered.

Sure, there were other elements of the purchase price, such as LinkedIn Learning. This was originally bought in 2015 for US$1.5bn as an off-the-shelf learning provider operating under the brand Lynda. com, after the founder Lynda Weinman. However, these were but peripheral luxuries within the proverbial Microsoft shopping basket.

Is Bill Gates (one of the globe's richest individuals, remember) really that stupid?

We're Going to Go on a Deep, Deep Dive

Let's rewind on LinkedIn history. We're going to go on a deep, deep dive. And it's a great story!

The genesis of LinkedIn starts, funnily enough, with a small network of people. Principal among these is majority shareholder and one of the key founders, Reid Hoffman. Hoffman was considered smart enough to receive an offer to join the main board of Microsoft postacquisition. Fortunately for Microsoft, he said yes, but we'll get to that a bit later.

Reid Hoffman is a very interesting man. And to a large extent, LinkedIn is Hoffman's baby.

Born in 1967 in the Palo Alto region of California, he is the son of two lawyers. Both played a part in the U.S. Civil Rights movement of the 1960s. Hoffman's egalitarian and libertarian influences started early.

Of course, this was well before #blacklivesmatter, but this reference point is still significant in the way Hoffman thinks. And let's face it, this is very much contrarian to the traditional image of Silicon Valley giants.

Hoffman was high school educated at the unusual choice of The Putney School. Unusual because the campus is approximately 3,000 miles away, where it enjoys the inclement climate of Vermont, bordering with Canada. Winter temperatures are described as too cold for snow or rain. Not exactly Palo Alto! Rumor has it that the young Reid chose the school himself and completed the application documents, only later telling his parents of his plans.

The Putney School has an enviable ethos. Attendees learn self-reliance, resilience, teamwork, and co-operation. When the school needed additional classrooms to be constructed, the students were involved in both the design and labor.

The school's motto, as penned by founder Carmelita Hinton, is "To treasure the stretching of oneself, to render service." Hoffman had chosen well.

Spin forward and the teenage Reid is found studying under the famed Symbolic Systems Program at Stanford University and, later, courtesy of a Marshall Scholarship, receiving a Master of Studies in Philosophy from Wolfson College, the University of Oxford, England.

Fresh from this intense study, Hoffman's dream at one point was to enter academia and become a "public intellectual." Again, very far removed from Silicon Valley.

Quite how Hoffman got from this point to LinkedIn is probably the subject of a whole book. Suffice to say, from an early LinkedIn-light where lessons of failure were learned, to LinkedIn's birth in 2003 involved a cast of characters and some classmates at Stanford. Referred to as the "PayPal Mafia," their number included Peter Thiel (cofounder of PayPal and nicknamed "the don") and Elon Musk.

The Economic Graph

An integral part of the LinkedIn business model is the Economic Graph. This is a massive dataset held by LinkedIn, which depicts individual members, job vacancies, skills, educational institutions, and so on. In essence, it's a digital representation of the global economy.

The word graph can have several meanings. To mathematicians, particularly those of the computational social science school, it is a diagram that shows nodes (or data points) and the relationship between them. The Economic Graph joins up real-world data in a way never before envisaged. Its purpose, worthy of any billionaire philosopher, is "To enable people to have as many transformative economic opportunities as possible."

We leave the LinkedIn world at this point to progress with the part played by data science in understanding how people networks "work" and how computers are used to model and analyze social phenomena.

The research of specialists such as Duncan J. Watts and Albert-László Barabási is greatly admired in their specialist field of computational social science but, frankly, deserves to be much better known.

Watts, in particular, has the unusual knack of making extremely complicated theories take on the properties of simple explanation. He is a rare combination of hardcore scientist and literary genius; his book, *Six Degrees: The Science of a Connected Age*, is a must-read.

The book title, of course, is an homage to the stage play and subsequent film of the same name. You probably know the story; we are but six steps from any other human on this planet. Even games are played to demonstrate this. If you are a movie buff, you may have heard of the fun challenge "Six degrees of Kevin Bacon" (the actor and, in my country at least, mobile phone promoter).

But you may not be aware that academic research into six degrees of connectivity has some involvement with the name Stanley Milgram. As every undergraduate psychology student knows, Milgram is famed for originating a mock electric shock experiment to highlight theories of obedience and, essentially, the "Man's inhumanity to man" horrors of Nazi Germany.

White-coated lab technicians urged participants to "administer" ever-higher levels of electric shock to absent and unharmed confederates who could then be heard over intercom screaming in agony. Fooling participants in this way is considered highly unethical today and has led to some questioning of the results Milgram obtained.

Milgram coined his own six steps research "the small world problem." The name comes from the way we humans express surprise when our contacts, values, hobbies, and so on are found to be the same as that of a complete stranger we've only just met at a dinner party: "It's a small world, isn't it?"

Except it isn't that strange. And it's been proven to be so. We really are much more connected than we think we are.

Watts' work, and that of others, takes these real-world problems (sound familiar, vis-à-vis the Economic Graph?) and provides explanations based on the massive data sets we are now fortunate to have access to, courtesy of a combination of cheap computing power and anonymized output from social media.

Eureka Moments …

Image © 2021 Daniel Byron

Eureka Moments Often Turn Out to Be Ephemeral

And these explanations, when delivered, invariably sound just like good old common sense. As Duncan Watts says, "by the time it gets out into the larger world … it takes on an aura of inevitability it never had in the making."

Eureka moments often turn out to be ephemeral. And ideas only have true explanatory power when people understand them fully.

Rather like a networker's elevator pitch, the content might be good, but we always need the right language to make it land effectively. Put another way, and using the title of Watts' later work, "Everything is Obvious: Once You Know the Answer."

I mentioned Microsoft's invitation for Reid Hoffman to join the main board. This was no accident or attempt to play to any vanity on the part of Hoffman.

No, Microsoft had already admitted to an image problem. And insider commentators knew they were looking to "clean up their act," mainly at the instigation of new CEO, Satya Nadella, appointed in 2014, just two years before the LinkedIn acquisition.

You see, Microsoft needed to change. And in all respects, including their less than favorable public image.

Picture the scene in the early 2010s. Microsoft's smartphone operation had flopped. The then CEO, Steve Balmer, perceived as a rather combative individual, had unfairly described the operating system Linux as a "cancer."

Linux was (and still is) not only free, open-source software and the antithesis of Microsoft's then sales model, it is also the favored choice of many an up-and-coming hip Valley programmer. Just the kind of people that Microsoft desperately needed to attract to grow and thrive.

Furthermore, for too many industry professionals, Microsoft represented a version of "the evil empire." Cross them and, if they couldn't sue you, they'd buy you!

Enter Nadella and the company changed. The whole shebang changed. And with this, a much softer, more collaborative version of Microsoft appeared.

It no longer wanted to be the cool company in the tech sector, but "the company that makes other people cool." Nadella also coined the phrase "Don't be a know-it-all. Be a learn-it-all."

Nadella's magic worked. In 2018, Microsoft became the most valuable company on the planet for the first time since 2002. It is still, of course, highly profitable.

The Real Reason ...

But this is a book about networking. And there's another twist to the story that requires us to reconsider Reid Hoffman and his connections within the hyper-everything world of Silicon Valley.

Hoffman is, of course, a consummate networker. But he's also a start-up investor par excellence and extremely well-respected in that community. America's record of funding start-ups is the envy of the world and something that many countries, mostly unsuccessfully, have tried to emulate.

Enviable because, whatever the economic shock, it always seems to find a way to bounce back. Its method of funding is a superb engine of growth and, indeed, something that has powered many a philanthropic project in the past. These have done many needy people much good.

So perhaps we are getting to the real reason why Microsoft handed over the US$26.2bn. They wanted to acquire a valuable network. And they got one.

It's a basic psychological principle that we are all judged by the company we keep. Reid understands this. Satya understands this. And Microsoft also understands this very well indeed.

Take Action

- Social media is not a panacea. Don't be a one club golfer. Also, the user interface can change quite rapidly. If you feel it would be a useful addition to your networking efforts, try to keep up to date on how to use it effectively.
- Use the same platform that, for example, your prospective mentor uses. Don't try to contact them on LinkedIn if they are an enthusiastic Tweeter.
- Utilize the potential of LinkedIn. Bill Gates doesn't normally spend US$26.2bn without good reason! Joining a LinkedIn group can be a great way to get in touch with like-minded souls. But you must engage!
- Ensure the number of LinkedIn connections you have is sufficient to leverage network effects.

CHAPTER 10

What Happens Next? (The NEXTworking Play)

Should we choose to Google networking, we'll find that an awful lot of the hits returned, relate to advice about networking events.

There's plenty of information out there about meeting people, engaging in small talk, moving on to an "elevator pitch" and, where necessary, making a swift exit from a conversation.

But focusing solely on the networking event itself might be misguided advice.

After all, while the initial contact is undoubtedly important, surely *what happens next* is where the real action (and opportunity) happens?

We can call this "NEXTworking."

NEXTworking—The Approach

Opportunity knocks …

Thomas Edison is quoted as saying "Opportunity is missed by most people because it is dressed in overalls and looks like work." If we want our networking to be successful, all of us must "do the work."

Let's assume we have met a new contact; the conversation has flowed well and we've had a positive response to a suggestion that we follow up.

Whether the follow up is a lunch, a cup of coffee, or a simple phone call, there are a few tried and tested strategies that are backed up by scientific research in the field of ethical influence and persuasion and behavioral science "nudge" techniques.

We discussed earlier that people (and particularly people who have influence) are busy. The sooner we can remind them of the initial meeting, reapply the context and respectfully move things forward, the better.

An early e-mail the next day will reposition us in their thoughts. Whatever commitment we may have regarding a call on their time needs to be posed as a question, not an assertion and certainly not a demand.

We could say "You agreed to meet me." But something along the lines of "I enjoyed our conversation and really would like to follow up. I'm free the week commencing x, would this work for you?" is likely to achieve a better outcome.

NEXTworking—The Conversation

So, let's say we have our meeting or phone call booked. The next stage is to think about the desired outcome. What does this look like? What do we want to achieve? What action would represent the next step in our strategy?

The eminent professor, Ed Schein of MIT Sloan, talks of "Humble Inquiry" as the gentle art of asking instead of telling. Humble inquiry is a process of talking tentatively. It means that our sentence construction is likely to include "Is it possible," "Could I," "Can I," and other phrases, which avoid assertions that might be perceived as dominant.

This approach is mirrored in Susan Cain's inspirational work on ensuring that power dynamics do not sabotage relationship building.

These valuable tips are included in Cain's "Ways to Use the Power of Powerless Communication":

1. Be humble but humorous. Cain gives the example of when the notoriously unphotogenic Abraham Lincoln was called "two-faced" during a debate. Lincoln is said to have replied: "Two-faced? If I had another face, do you think I would wear this one?"

2. Pair openness with competence. A revealing experiment tracked audience reactions to participants in a game show. When the high-performing contestants spilt coffee on themselves, the audience liked them more. They were competent, yet also relatable: human and imperfect.

   But when the mediocre performers did the same thing, people liked them less. The takeaway: if we're doing our job well, people want us to be human. It's when we're underperforming that powerless communication backfires.

3. When we communicate with someone, we should ask ourselves three questions: What do we have to learn from them? How can *we* help *them* (or otherwise express warmth toward them)? And can we find ways of letting our true personality show?

4. Frame our opinions as suggestions. "I wonder if it would work to do it this way." Give people the space to disagree. This is another example of tentative talk.

As a final point, Cain urges women in the corporate world to follow their natural inclinations. Women tend naturally to use powerless communication styles. Rather than worry that this is a bad thing in a take-charge, push, and shove world, Cain offers encouragement to use the style effectively.

Implementing NEXTworking

Let's cover how we might implement our NEXTworking strategy. Whether our contact can advise on freelance work, how to expand our client base or guide us on a permanent position, the underlying touch points for the conversation are similar.

In his book *The 2-Hour Job Search*, career and employment specialist Steve Dalton talks about building conversational questions around the TIARA technique. Here are some examples of this questioning approach:

Trends—What's happening in the industry right now? What's hot and what's not?

Insights—Doing what you do, is there anything that surprises you? What path took you to where you are now? This is how things appear to me—are they the same for you?

Advice—Note, the technique is to ask for advice not help. As covered earlier, this is because, compared to advice, information, or guidance, help is a whole different ballgame. Help can imply helplessness on our part (not necessarily a good thing) and a big, potentially guilt-ridden, obligation on the part of the helpee. This is very tricky territory that is best avoided.

Resources—This is a question about whether we have missed anything. But it's important here to impress on the other party that we haven't come to the meeting cold. In other words, we've done our homework. So rather than say "Do you have any contacts I should speak with?" it's better we say "I've researched A, B and C and spoken with X and Y. What I've deduced from this is Z. Is there anything or anyone I might add to this?"

Assignments—This is where the subtlety kicks in. Getting a full-time gig or a permanent commitment is tricky for prospective clients or employers. Business is tough and a long-term overhead in an uncertain commercial world is a big ask. Far better is a "try before you buy" strategy of finding out what short-term projects or assignments might be coming up. What's under development? What plans can be shared?

In all interactions, we should beware of prying into commercial confidentiality. We should also avoid the temptation to jump in if we perceive an opportunity. Rather than say immediately "I can help with that!," the best practice is to take note and store up the information for the future.

Used in the right way, TIARA can provide a very powerful guiding framework for conversations with network contacts.

Influence and Persuasion

Over 30 years ago, a young psychology academic decided to take a sabbatical. But not in the form of a holiday.

In pursuit of an interest in how people are influenced, he set off to work undercover in several occupations, such as insurance clerk, second-hand car salesman, and real estate vendor.

What Robert Cialdini, now professor of Psychology and Marketing at Arizona State University, discovered were six guiding principles. These were published in his 1984 seminal work, *Influence: The Psychology of Persuasion*.

Cialdini sets out the principles as follows:

Likeability—Being perceived as likeable by others is a big plus to relationships. Likeability is of sufficient interest to be covered in a later chapter in the book (see Troubleshooting—For When Our Networking is Notworking).

Consistency—People we interact with generally appreciate consistency of behavior on our part. As an individual, if we continue to fit their internal model of us, there is less conflict and more comfort.

Reciprocity—If we've ever received a free pen in a mailing from a charity or life insurance company, this is the application of the principle of reciprocity. In short, if someone does something for us, we will be minded to do something for them.

Authority—A friend volunteers some of her spare time as a "Special Constable" in the UK Police Force. She often remarks on how differently people treat her when she is "in uniform," as opposed to being out of it. Of course, there are many other forms of authority beyond what we wear—official titles for example or even the way we speak.

Scarcity—Known to all retailers worldwide, "Buy now while stocks last" is a perfect example of scarcity as a tool of persuasion.

Social Proof—As social animals, we have evolved to make use of the opinions of others rather than expend time and effort finding things out for ourselves. What others do serves as a useful guide to what we should also do. So, as people, we are persuaded by the actions of others. Examples abound within comparison websites and the rating devices used whenever we buy a good or service.

We are not saying, for example, that scarcity works by saying "If I don't get a job from you now, I'll be snapped up by someone else next week!" To put forward an ultimatum in this way would clearly be relationship threatening.

But to know Cialdini's principles is useful, even if there is a degree of subtlety in their application to our networking efforts.

Behavioral Insights (The Nudge Play)

The burgeoning science of behavioral insights has been catapulted into public consciousness through the work of the UK government's former "nudge" unit and the book of the same name authored by Professor Richard Thaler and Cass Sunstein.

Behavioral insights, or "nudges," examine how "choice architecture" can be fashioned to subtly move people in the desired direction. Dr. David Halpern, Chief Executive of the UK's Behavioural Insights Team (BIT), elegantly defines a nudge as "a means of encouraging or guiding behaviour, but without mandating or instructing."

The advertising world has been nudging us since the industry first came into being. Try saying "Beanz, meanz ... ," without hearing the word Heinz in your head to conclude the advertising strapline. This is a nudge!

It's important to remember that nudges are for the greater good and need to be employed in an ethical manner. Nudging is not about manipulating people against their will—even if such a thing were possible in a mentee/mentor context.

There's a useful mnemonic developed by the BIT through the scientific study of what works when nudging. This is "EAST," which stands for Easy, Attractive, Social, and Timely.

Make it **Easy**—Simplifying messages and smoothing processes are both elements of making it easy for people to deal with us.

For someone to be conscious of something, they first need to attend to it. This is not as easy as it sounds in a world of significant background "noise."

So, the first challenge is to find a creative way to bring our message to conscious attention. We need to do this by first understanding how to communicate and then getting to work on finessing our message and being crystal clear on what it is we do and how we bring value to the table.

Making it easy is also about harnessing the power of defaults. Essentially, it's about turning the question on its head: "Would you want to work with me?" becomes "Why would you NOT want to work with me?"

Make it **Attractive**—Our messages may make absolute sense and be expertly crafted. But do they engage people and draw them toward us?

Remember the three key areas we discussed under "How to Craft Our Key Messages": When we drill down deep into our motivations, this automatically provides insight into why we do what we do, and what it means to us. And, as we have said, this starts to make us realize our feelings for what we do.

And tapping into these "just are" feelings is so very much more powerful and engaging than spilling out the thoughts we have.

We just don't need to go there with thoughts. Feelings are so much easier to use as a communication tool and as a means of achieving one of our key objectives—having people remember us!

Make it **Social**—People are persuaded by the actions of others. We should, therefore, harness the goodwill from our reserve of supporters and cheerleaders.

When we make this goodwill known to prospective mentors, we actively demonstrate that we are trusted by others. They can be encouraged to join this throng.

We can let a prospective mentor know that our adviser network includes other noteworthy people. This allows them to share in the pro-social behaviors of others and they will identify with this good practice.

We can even consider introducing mentors to each other, if appropriate, to share and leverage the goodwill across our network.

Make it **Timely**—Consider approaching mentors when the time is right.

Is there a point at which our own value as a prospective mentee is maximized (perhaps the mentor might welcome a review of a recently published book)?

Again, we can think about events where Q&A sessions are part of the proceedings. These opportunities can provide privileged access to those we wouldn't normally mix with.

If we pose a well-prepared and insightful question, this can provide a platform to continue the dialogue later. The mentor will remember us for the right reasons.

Developing a mentor network can be tricky. Utilizing behavioral insights in an ethical and authentic way might just provide the help we need. "Nudging" works!

NEXTworking Is Just as Important as Networking (The NEXTworking Play)

It's important for us to know how to meet and greet people effectively to build our personal brand and become known.

But what happens next shouldn't be ignored. It's often where the real relationship building is done and where long-term and mutually beneficial partnerships are forged.

Talking tentatively, using appreciative inquiry and employing powerless communication are all techniques that can help position us as someone worth knowing. As such, our social capital is enhanced.

If we can couple these techniques with Cialdini's reflections on influence and persuasion and build in what we know to work from behavioral insights, we have a winning combination!

Take Action

- Don't waste time and effort by failing to follow up.
- Ed Schein's humble inquiry, Susan Cain's powerless communication, and Steve Dalton's TIARA method are all useful tools.
- Cialdini's influence and persuasion principles and EAST can add to your toolkit.

CHAPTER 11

When Our Networking Is NOT Working (The Troubleshooting Play)

Networking is never a short-term fix. Rather, it's a habit that needs to be formed through the practice of good principles.

But we can all recognize situations where try as we might, it seems particularly hard to make our networking strategy work for us.

Maybe we've hit a bit of a block? Maybe the approaches we've made to potential contacts and prospective mentors have come to nothing?

Here are some thoughts about dealing with this.

Network Smart (The Stew Play)

The ideas of Wharton professor, Stew Friedman promote four dimensions in our lives: Work, Family, Society, and Self.

His Better Leader, Richer Life program has identified that a more desirable balance across the four domains leads to improved performance in our professional lives. It's as if the revised perspective in terms of what is truly important for an individual allows greater clarity and commitment in the professional domain.

Being smart in the use of time across the domains is also a strategy for personal effectiveness. For example, taking part in a charity corporate social responsibility event involving a fun run could potentially provide multiple benefits in all four dimensions. It could deliver engagement with colleagues outside of a work context, improved standing within the organization, advantages for the community, health benefits, and, if children or family are involved, a shared positive experience in the family domain.

If we can find networking opportunities that generate a "four-way win," we'll be making really good use of our time.

Being Lucky (The Wiseman Play)

Scientists have found that "lucky" people are no different from the rest of us. Research undertaken by Professor Richard Wiseman shows they simply adopt a more open attitude and therefore "consistently encounter chance opportunities."

Professor Wiseman's book cites the case of the multimillion lottery winner who considered themselves "unlucky." Why? Because they had to share their winnings with someone else who picked out the same random number. Unlucky, because they could have won more as a sole winner!

Similarly, the unfortunate bank cashier caught in an armed raid, shot in the arm, and seriously wounded. Here they feel just how "lucky" they are. The bullet might have been higher.

Over 30 years ago, the eminent psychologist Alfred Bandura noted that "some of the most important determinants of life's paths often arise through the most trivial of circumstances."

Personality studies suggest those who perceive themselves as unlucky are generally more tense and anxious. Furthermore, this anxiety can disrupt the ability to notice the unexpected. Too many become locked into a focus that can cause us to miss out on the activity around us.

The trick is to keep open to opportunity. And be ready to learn. Anything.

We should also bear in mind that "lucky" people benefit from another skill.

They carry a clear and consistent dialogue in their heads which, when called upon, explains quickly and memorably who they are and what their career project entails. In other words, they have a laser-like image of their broad direction of travel.

If we don't have this kind of internal story worked out and ready to deliver at a moment's notice, there's some very good advice: We should all commit ourselves as soon as possible to construct one!

Being Likeable (The Networking Niceties Play)

We know that being perceived as likeable when meeting people is a big plus. We'll recall that likeability is one of the six influence and persuasion principles identified in Dr. Robert Cialdini's work.

But if we weren't fortunate enough to be born under a guiding and gilded star, how can we go about being likeable?

Well, there are certain things we can do. Let's call these Networking Niceties.

- Smile! The smile, when used as a component of a first impression, is a world beater. In Dr. Heidi Grant's book, eye contact, nodding, and smiling are listed as the three key physical indicators of warmth.
- At the start of any conversation, we should try to listen more than talk. Remember the technique of reflecting. This prompts the other party to open up further on the topic. People generally appreciate being given the conversational space to tell their personal story.
- If a one-to-one conversation with the boss is going well enough to press our case for promotion, don't ask for help. Instead, ask for advice. Remember the four benefits that advice seeking brings: Learning; Perspective Taking; Flattery; Commitment.
- If it's difficult to be agreeable to the person we are interacting with, then we should try not to be disagreeable. Respect others' point of view, whether we warm to it or not. If we are not feeling on top form and therefore perhaps a little irritable, take a moment, and try to relax. Don't let it damage our Playbook. We'll feel better for it.
- Step forward, don't step back. This is a great technique known to many professional actors as a key element of stagecraft. Perhaps we've been asked a question to which we don't know the answer? How do we react? Most of us automatically take a step back and literally "go on the back foot." The alternative is to lean in toward the person posing the question and say something like:

"I don't know, but I'd be interested in the answer!"

Or;

"That's really interesting, I've never thought of it that way."

A simple action, but one that has potential to position us in a much more positive and likeable light.

If all of this sounds a bit too touchy-feely, we've hit upon an interesting paradox.

We can engage in certain behaviors to be likeable, but when we want to appear competent we often do the opposite. Whether through nervous energy or getting carried away in the moment, we tend to speak more than listen, overfocus on our own accomplishments and demonstrate our expertise by challenging the views of others. (If this sounds a bit like Social Media, you are right!)

The answer is to emphasize those elements of our behavior that don't risk being labeled as fluffy, lacking rationale and perhaps uninformed, but nonetheless highlight the moral aspects of personal warmth.

We can do this by demonstrating traits such as fairness, honesty, and responsibility, all of which build trust with other people.

Speaking (The Speaking Play)

Speaking in front of other people can be a great networking tool. Why? Because it can have the effect of drawing people toward us. It's that same "pull." This is so much more effective than the blatant "push" that so many folks feel they must employ to be noticed. Surely we can be more subtle than that?

Now, some people call this "Public Speaking." But we might want to shy away from that term and everything it implies.

No, we should perhaps prefer to call it "Speaking in front of friends who we haven't yet met." Any psychologists reading this will now be enjoying a wry smile, because they have "twigged" what we've just done to calm any nerves!

We can certainly speak. Many of us have done so since a very early age.* We can certainly speak with other people (although not everyone does, but that perhaps is the subject of another book!).

And we can certainly speak in front of other people. Why should going up to a raised platform or standing in front of a dais make any difference?

But this isn't a book that covers how to speak with other people, so we'll leave it there apart from a couple of references.

The very wonderful Caroline Goyder teaches people to speak with gravitas. Indeed, this single word is the title of Caroline's book. Caroline worked at London's famed Central School of Speech and Drama as a voice coach for over 10 years. She is a lovely person who helps others.

Another equally lovely person in the same mold is Ges Ray. Ges lives outside of London in his country mansion and, among other things, is a world-class singer who has performed at many top venues, including New York's Carnegie Hall.

Ges has developed a range of resources for those interested in this topic. One particularly useful one is his pocket-book "Speak Performance." The beauty of the pocket book is we can take it with us wherever we go. If we are called upon even to make an impromptu speech, the book is at hand to guide and advise. Brilliant!

I used to have the task of phoning a particularly challenging client. He would answer and I, being polite and wanting to make sure he was free, would ask "Can you speak?"

He would always reply "Of course. I've been able to since a baby." After a couple of times exposure to this rather feeble attempt at a joke, I learned my lesson. I just used to email him instead!

Try Not to Stress (The Twain Play)

Mark Twain (he of Huckleberry Finn fame), when referring to our natural ability to imagine negative consequences, said: "I am an old man and have known a great many troubles, but most of them never happened."

So, we should have faith in our own ability.

Things that take on the highest urgency and importance today will be viewed as insignificant trifles in years to come. It's only a question of perception. If we reframe problems as challenges or opportunities, we'll start to see that we can't fail, only learn.

Cultivating a Professional Mindset (The Professional Play)

Sometimes we must accept that we are going through a rough patch with our networking. But tough times don't last for long and they always teach us something about ourselves.

If we retain our professional outlook and hold on to the right values, we'll pull through.

In this edited extract, Shane Parrish of Farnham Street blog has some worthwhile thoughts on how professionals differ from amateurs:

- Amateurs stop when they achieve something. Professionals understand the initial achievement is just the beginning.
- Amateurs don't have any idea what improves the odds of achieving good outcomes. Professionals do.
- Amateurs focus on identifying their weaknesses and improving them. Professionals focus on their strengths and on finding people who are strong where they are weak.
- Amateurs think withholding knowledge is power. Professionals pass on wisdom and advice.
- Amateurs focus on being right. Professionals focus on getting the best outcome.
- Amateurs focus on the short term. Professionals focus on the long term.
- Amateurs go faster. Professionals go further.
- Amateurs value isolated performance. Professionals value consistency.
- Amateurs have a goal. Professionals have a process.

Makin' Whoopee?

Speaking at an event can have its benefits, as discussed. As I have said many times, it's a great way to exert the "pull," rather than have to "push."

But just beware. When you exit the stage, you may have a build-up of adrenalin in your body. This is a perfectly natural by-product of getting "up" to deliver a kind of performance. And the effect may be stronger if you are toward the introversion end of the personality scale.

This adrenalin can occasionally affect your judgment. The event host might offer a refreshing alcoholic beverage to "calm us down" or even just as a thank you. It's a perfectly natural thing for them to do in the spirit of being grateful for what you have done.

The problem is, at this point, the brain doesn't need alcohol. It's a known dehydrating drug. What it really needs is a good long glass of cool water to rehydrate and, thereby, make the most of the golden opportunity for networking that "Speaking in front of friends who we haven't yet met" offers all of us.

So, politely refuse the alcohol and ask for a glass of water instead.

Poor judgment can also lead to other things, but I'll leave the lyricist Gus Kahn and songwriter Walter Donaldson (another great network) to call this one out to all genders.

(Please bear in mind that, within this extract, the lyrics are of their time and do not reflect my personal views or the mores of today. By the way, in my opinion, one of the best renditions of this song is the Great American Songbook Volume IV version, performed by those two august knights of the realm, Sir Rod Stewart and Sir Elton John).

Makin' Whoopee (Kahn and Donaldson 1928)

Another bride, another June
Another sunny honeymoon
Another season, another reason
For makin' whoopee
A lot of shoes, a lot of rice
The groom is nervous, he answers twice
It's really killin'
That he's so willin' to make whoopee
Now picture a little love nest
Down where the roses cling
Picture the same sweet love nest
Think what a year can bring, yes
He's washin' dishes and baby clothes
He's so ambitious he even sews

But don't forget folks
That's what you get folks, for makin' whoopee
Another year, maybe less
What's this I hear? Well, can't you guess?
She feels neglected, and he's suspected
Of makin' whoopee
Yeah, she sits alone
Most every night
He doesn't phone, he doesn't write
He says he's busy
But she says, "is he?"
He's makin' whoopee

Take Action

- Stew Friedman's four dimensions, thinking "lucky" and Networking Niceties will fix our networking automobile when it stalls on the highway.
- Being a speaker can pay dividends.
- Don't stress. In four hours, four days, four weeks, or four years, it won't matter.
- Be professional in word and deed.

CHAPTER 12

A Final Word ...
(Are We Agile or Fragile?—
the Final Play)

We mentioned earlier in the book, the adage "If you don't go, you'll never know!"

For some of us, practicing our face-to-face networking technique in a live environment may involve some anxiety, discomfort, and personal risk.

In a modern world where the word "agility" is used a lot, perhaps we need to ask ourselves "Are we agile, or fragile?"

But help is at hand from the "gratitude attitude": Be a generous networker. Let's consider other people at the event who may be feeling as anxious as we are. Let's focus on what can be done to help them feel more comfortable. Again, this is a great tool for taking the pressure off us.

One of my personal motivations for writing this book was to ensure that any observations, thoughts, or recommendations for *your* Playbook are supported by robust science.

In other words, I have tried to employ the evidence-based approach favored by Professor Rob Briner and colleagues at the Center for Evidence Based Management (www.cebma.org). More specifically, it is "a management approach that involves using multiple sources of scientific evidence and empirical results as a means of attaining knowledge."

Please forgive me then if I finish with some more science:

Research at the University of Rochester has identified that "having few social connections is equivalent to tobacco use" (Carmichael et al. 2015).

Put another way, social contact has long been known as a positive factor in good health and longevity. This sounds like sound advice: It was for the best of reasons that a well-meaning friend once said to me, "You've got to get out more!"

It's my sincere hope that you have enjoyed this book and that you are ready to give people networking a go (or, if you've tried it before with limited success, give it another go!)

You may have the perception of me as some sharp-suited, silver-tongued snake oil salesperson. I can assure you that nothing could be further from the truth! Another personal motivation for writing the book was to allow you to learn from my mistakes and, partly or completely, take the journey that I have taken to try to improve.

Our LinkedIn group (Strategic Business Networking/Networking Playbook) is currently over 500 members strong. The group is designed to share actionable thoughts around people networking and to work together to consider key questions or points of interest on the same theme. Everything is free to members.

Do join us!

Deciding how to close a book can be tricky. Let me end where we started, with that extract from why our Group exists:

We're a Q&A forum to ask questions and share best practice. We're for anyone who is looking to improve their people networking skills to enjoy a better career, improved working relationships, and a happier working life.

Being strategic in your networking isn't about Machiavellian sharp practice, deceit, or political maneuvering. Instead, it's about starting with the end in mind, thinking about what you want to achieve and having an ethical route map to get there.

Networking is not a nil sum game (win/lose). Instead, it's about making the pie bigger in terms of opportunities. Let's work together and make the pie as big as possible!

References and Further Reading

Preface

Pettman, D. 2009. "Love in the Time of Tamagotchi." *Theory, Culture & Society* 26, nos. 2–3, 189–208. https://doi.org/10.1177/0263276409103117 (accessed June 07, 2021).

Introduction

Covey, S.R. 1989. *The 7 Habits of Highly Effective People. Powerful Lessons in Personal Change.* New York, NY: Simon & Schuster, Inc.

McKeown, G. 2021. "Stephen R. Covey Taught Me Not to Be Like Him." *Harvard Business Review,* https://hbr.org/2012/07/stephen-r-covey-taught-me-not?registration=success (accessed June 07, 2021).

Chapter 1

Human Values Foundation: https://humanvaluesfoundation.com/

Playbook definition: Oxford English Dictionary. *OxfordLanguages.* https://languages.oup.com/dictionaries/#oed (accessed June 07, 2021).

Professor Roy Porter quote from: "In Our Time: The Enlightenment in Britain." *British Broadcasting Corporation: BBC Radio 4.* www.bbc.co.uk/programmes/p005479m (accessed June 07, 2021).

Uzzi, B. 2021. "Research: Men and Women Need Different Kinds of Networks to Succeed." *Harvard Business Review.* https://hbr.org/2019/02/research-men-and-women-need-different-kinds-of-networks-to-succeed (accessed August 09, 2021).

Yang, Y., N.V. Chawla, and B. Uzzi. 2019. "A Network's Gender Composition and Communication Pattern Predict Women's Leadership Success." *Proceedings of the National Academy of Sciences* 116, no. 6, 2033–2038. https://doi.org/10.1073/pnas.1721438116

Chapter 2

Chitty, M. 2021. "First, Second and Third Sectors—The Unrealised Opportunities." *WordPress: Progressive Managers' Network. Managing People with Passion.* https://progmanager.wordpress.com/2007/10/02/first-second-and-third-sectors-the-unrealised-opportunities/ (accessed March 23, 2021).

Granovetter, M.S. 1973. "The Strength of Weak Ties." *American Journal of Sociology* 78, no. 6, 1360–1380. www.jstor.org/stable/2776392 (accessed June 07, 2021).

Grant, A.M. 2013. *Give and Take: A Revolutionary Approach to Success.* New York, NY: Viking.

Grant, A. 2021. "In the Company of Givers and Takers." *Harvard Business Review*, https://hbr.org/2013/04/in-the-company-of-givers-and-takers (accessed June 07, 2021).

Putnam, R.D. 2000. *Bowling Alone: The Collapse and Revival of American Community.* New York, NY: Simon & Schuster, Inc.

Chapter 3

Bolton, G. 2009. "Write to Learn: Reflective Practice Writing." *Innovait: Education And Inspiration for General Practice* 2, no. 12, 752–754. https://journals.sagepub.com/doi/10.1093/innovait/inp105

Cattell, R.B. 1950. *An Introduction to Personality Study.* London, England: Routledge, Taylor & Francis Group.

Clance, P.R., and S.A. Imes. 1978. "The Imposter Phenomenon in High Achieving Women: Dynamics and Therapeutic Intervention." *Psychotherapy: Theory, Research & Practice* 15, no. 3, 241–247. https://doi.org/10.1037/h0086006

Collins English Dictionary. 2005. Seventh Edition. Glasgow, United Kingdom: HarperCollins Publishers.

Dweck, C.S. 2006. *Mindset: The New Psychology of Success.* New York, NY: Random House.

Fletcher, B.C., and K.J. Pine. 2012. *Flex: Do Something Different.* Hatfield, England: University of Hertfordshire Press.

Grant, A.M. 2021. *Think Again: The Power of Knowing What You Don't Know.* New York, NY: Viking, an imprint of Penguin Random House LLC.

Hammond, M. 2021. "Education Studies; Reflexivity." *The University of Warwick.* https://warwick.ac.uk/fac/soc/ces/research/current/socialtheory/maps/reflexivity/ (accessed June 08, 2021).

Little, B.R. 2014. *Me, Myself, and Us: The Science of Personality and the Art of Well-Being.* Philadelphia, PA: Perseus Books.

More on 'acting out of character' from Adam Grant (based on the theories of Brian Little): Grant, A. 2018. "Your Hidden Personality." *Work Life Podcast Audio, Season 1.*

On reflexivity: Reflexivity. *Google Arts & Culture.* https://artsandculture.google.com/entity/r%C3%A9flexivit%C3%A9/m0b8b_5 (accessed June 08, 2021).

Peters, S. 2012. *The Chimp Paradox.* London, England: Vermilion.

Senge, P.M. 1990. *The Fifth Discipline: The Art and Practice of the Learning Organization.* New York, NY: Doubleday/Currency.

Winterman, D. 2021. "Rumination: The Danger of Dwelling." *BBC News Magazine (Online).* www.bbc.co.uk/news/magazine-24444431

Chapter 4

Dunbar, R. 2010. *How Many Friends Does One Person Need?: Dunbar's Number and Other Evolutionary Quirks.* London, England: Faber and Faber Ltd.

Misner, I. 2021. "Premature Solicitation." *Dr Ivan Misner: Business Networking and More.* https://ivanmisner.com/premature-solicitation/ (accessed June 08, 2021).

Chapter 5

Breakwell, G.M., S.E. Hammond, C.E. Fife-Schaw, and J.A. Smith, Jonathan. 2006. *Research Methods in Psychology*, 3rd ed. London, England: Sage Publications Ltd.

Grant, A.M. 2016. *Originals: How Non-Conformists Move the World.* New York, NY: Viking.

Heath, C. Winter 2003. "Loud and Clear; Crafting Messages that Stick—What Nonprofits Can Learn from Urban Legends." *Stanford Social Innovation Review*, https://ssir.org/articles/entry/loud_and_clear (accessed June 08, 2021).

Lopata, A. 2020. *Just Ask: Why Seeking Support is Your Greatest Strength.* St Albans, England: Panoma Press Ltd.

Newton, E.L. 1990. "Overconfidence in the Communication of Intent: Heard and Unheard Melodies." [Unpublished Ph.D. Dissertation] Stanford University.

Chapter 6

Arden, D. 2015. *Win Win: How to Get a Winning Result from Persuasive Negotiations.* Harlow, England: Pearson Education Ltd.

Simon Sinek's TED talk: Sinek, Simon. How Great Leaders Inspire Action. *TED, Ideas Worth Spreading*. www.ted.com/talks/simon_sinek_how_great_leaders_inspire_action (accessed March 09, 2021).

Townsend, H. 2015. *Poised for Partnership: From Senior Associate and Senior Manager to Partner by Building a Cast-Iron Business and Personal Case to Make Partner in Any Firm*. London, England: The Excedia Group.

Waldman, J. 2021. "Cutting Edge Career Advice—Since 2009." *Joshua Waldman's Career Enlightenment*. https://careerenlightenment.com/ (accessed June 08, 2021).

Woodford, Ted. 2021. Twoodfrd Channel. YouTube. www.youtube.com/channel/UC8wIqZCt9h6uJbOBCQVuUmg

Chapter 7

Dunbar, R. 2010. *How Many Friends Does One Person Need?: Dunbar's Number and Other Evolutionary Quirks*. London, England: Faber and Faber Ltd.

Eysenck, H.J. 1947. *Dimensions of Personality*. London, England: Kegan Paul, Trench, Trubner & Co., Ltd.

Ibarra, H., and M.L. Hunter. 2021. "How Leaders Create and Use Networks." *Harvard Business Review*. https://hbr.org/2007/01/how-leaders-create-and-use-networks (accessed May 01, 2021).

Little, B.R. 2014. *Me, Myself, and Us: The Science of Personality and the Art of Well-Being*. Philadelphia, PA: Perseus Books.

McKeown, G. 2021. "99% of Networking Is a Waste of Time." *Harvard Business Review*. https://hbr.org/2015/01/99-of-networking-is-a-waste-of-time (accessed June 06, 2021).

Professor Little's TED talk: Little, B. 2021. "Who are You, Really? The Puzzle of Personality." *TED, Ideas Worth Spreading*. www.ted.com/talks/brian_little_who_are_you_really_the_puzzle_of_personality?utm_campaign=tedspread-a&utm_medium=referral&utm_source=tedcomshare (accessed March 09, 2021).

Chapter 8

Franklin, B. (Published posthumously. Date unknown). *Autobiography of Benjamin Franklin: 1706-1757*. Bedford, MA: Applewood Books.

Grant, H. 2021. "A Second Chance to Make the Right Impression." *Harvard Business Review*. https://hbr.org/2015/01/a-second-chance-to-make-the-right-impression (accessed June 08, 2021).

Grant, H.H. 2015. *No One Understand You: and What to Do About It. Boston*, MA: Harvard Business School Publishing.

Kruse, K. 2021. "The Lost Art of Asking For Help (And How To Master It)." *Forbes*. www.forbes.com/sites/kevinkruse/2018/08/20/the-lost-art-of-asking-for-help-and-how-to-master-it/?sh=62a866f2f884 (accessed June 08, 2021).

Simon, P. 1986. "You Can Call Me Al." Track 6 on "Graceland." Warner Bros. Records, Vinyl record. Words and music by Paul Simon.

Simon, P., and A. Garfunkel. 1970. "Bridge over Troubled Water." *Columbia Records*, Vinyl record. Words and music by Paul Simon, except for "El Cóndor Pasa (If I Could)"; by Daniel Alomía Robles, arranged by Jorge Milchberg and English lyrics by Paul Simon, and "Bye Bye Love"; by Felice Bryant, Boudleaux Bryant.

Chapter 9

Barabási, A.L. 2003. *Linked: How Everything is Connected to Everything Else and What it Means for Business, Science, and Everyday Life*. New York, NY: Plume.

Dayton, A. 2021. "5 Tips to Game the LinkedIn Algorithm." *Forbes*, www.forbes.com/sites/adriandayton/2020/08/12/5-tips-to-game-the-linkedin-algorithm/ (accessed April 01, 2021).

Kipling, R. 2001. "If." *Collected Poems of Rudyard Kipling*, ed. R.T. Jones, 605. London, England: Wordsworth Editions.

McLuhan, M. 1964. *Understanding Media: The Extensions of Man*. New York, NY: McGraw-Hill.

Milgram, S. 1974. *Obedience to Authority: An Experimental View*. New York, NY: Harper & Row.

Morse, G. 2021. "The Science Behind Six Degrees." *Harvard Business Review*. https://hbr.org/2003/02/the-science-behind-six-degrees#:~:text=The%20notion%20of%20six%20degrees,by%20just%20a%20few%20intermediaries (accessed June 08, 2021).

Munir, S. 2021. "Beginner's Guide on How to Beat LinkedIn Algorithm." *Social Champ*, LinkedIn Marketing. www.socialchamp.io/blog/linkedin-algorithms-to-keep-in-mind-this-year/ (accessed June 08, 2021).

Sehl, K. 2021. "How the LinkedIn Algorithm Works and How to Make it Work for You." *Hootsuite Blog*, https://blog.hootsuite.com/how-the-linkedin-algorithm-works-hacks/ (accessed June 08, 2021).

Watts, D.J. 2003. *Six Degrees: The Science of a Connected Age*. New York, NY: Norton.

Watts, D.J. 2011. *Everything is Obvious Once You Know the Answer: How Common Sense Fails Us*. New York, NY: Crown Business.

Chapter 10

Cain, S. 2021. "7 Ways to Use the Power of Powerless Communication." *Susan Cain's Newsletter.* www.quietrev.com/7-ways-to-use-powerless-communication/

Cain, S. July 19, 2012. "The Power of the Introvert in Your Office." *HBR Ideacast. Harvard Business Review Podcast.* Episode 310. https://hbr.org/podcast/2012/07/the-power-of-the-introvert-in.html

Cialdini, R.B. 2007. *Influence: The Psychology of Persuasion.* New York, NY: Harper Business.

Dalton, S. 2012. *The 2-Hour Job Search: Using Technology to get the Right Job Faster.* Berkeley, CA: Ten Speed Press.

Halpern, D. 2015. *Inside the Nudge Unit: how small changes can make a big difference.* London, England: WH Allen.

Halpern, D. April 01, 2017. "Changing the World, One Nudge at a Time." *Harvard Business Publishing: Education,* https://hbsp.harvard.edu/product/ROT332-PDF-ENG (accessed June 08, 2021).

Schein, E.H., and P.A. Schein. n.d. *Humble inquiry: the gentle art of asking instead of telling.* Oakland, CA: Berrett-Koehler Publishers, Inc.

Thaler, R.H., and C.R. Sunstein. 2009. *Nudge: Improving Decisions About Health, Wealth, and Happiness.* New Haven, CT: Yale University Press.

Chapter 11

Bandura, A. 1998. "Exploration of Fortuitous Determinants of Life Paths." *Psychological Inquiry* 9, no. 2, 95–99. www.jstor.org/stable/1449098?seq=1

Friedman, S.D. April 2008. "Be a Better Leader, Have a Richer Life." *Harvard Business Review,* https://hbr.org/2008/04/be-a-better-leader-have-a-richer-life (accessed June 08, 2021).

Goyder, C. 2014. *Gravitas: Communicate with Confidence, Influence and Authority.* London, England: Vermilion.

Kahn, G., and W. Donaldson. 1928. *Makin' Whoopee.* Donaldson, Douglas & Gumble. Chapter 12

Parrish, S. "The Difference Between Amateurs and Professionals." *Farnham Street blog.* https://fs.blog/2017/08/amateurs-professionals/ (accessed June 08, 2021).

Ray, G. 2019. *Speak Performance: How to be a Confident, Compelling and Convincing Speaker.* Milton Keynes, United Kingdom: mPowr (Publishing) Ltd.

Wiseman, R. 2004. *The Luck Factor: The Scientific Study of the Lucky Mind.* London, England: Arrow Books Ltd.

Chapter 12

Carmichael, C.L., H.T. Reis, and P.R. Duberstein. March 2015. "In Your 20s it's Quantity, in Your 30s it's Quality: The Prognostic Value of Social Activity Across 30 Years of Adulthood." *Psychol and Aging* 30, no. 1, 95–105. http://doi.org.10.1037/pag0000014

Barends, E., and D.M. Rousseau. 2018. *Evidence-Based Management: How to Use Evidence to Make Better Organizational Decisions.* London, England: Kogan Page Ltd.

Additional Resources

The Strategic Business Networking LinkedIn Group can be found at: www.linkedin.com/groups/8430203

The Strategic Business Networking YouTube Channel can be found at: www.youtube.com/channel/UCX1NAvWBKUSEgibCrImtCoQ

For all other information, search www.darrylhowes.com

About the Author

Darryl L. Howes, MSc, is a learning and development consultant in the field of people networking and B2B relationship management. He has extensive experience of commercial value generation across a wide scope of consultancy assignments. Darryl's clients have ranged from UK Premier League Soccer Clubs to international financial services brands such as Barclays, Lloyds Banking Group, Santander, and Coutts.

This practical experience is underpinned by an evidence-based approach, employing behavioral science, and established research in the field of influence and persuasion. Darryl holds a 1st Class Honors degree in Psychology and a Masters in I-O Psychology from the University of Surrey, UK.

A published technical author, he also speaks, writes, and consults on Strategic Business Networking©, the abundance mindset, and social capital. He has written for The Chartered Institute of Personnel and Development, The Chartered Institute of Management Accountants, The Institute of Leadership and Management, and the Institute of Directors.

As a coach and mentor, he has guided others to success via his work with The Prince's Trust, Young Enterprise and Her Majesty The Queen's UK Commonwealth-wide Queen's Young Leaders Programme.

Darryl has been married to Debbie for over 40 years and cites this partnership as his most productive network. A keen amateur musician, he is continuing his attempts to smuggle home "just one more guitar" …

Index

alliteration, 57
Amazon-light model, 76
analogy, 57–58
Arden, D., 53
authority, 101

Bandura, A., 106
Barabási, A. L., 93
behavioral insights, 102–104
Benjamin Franklin effect (BF play),
    74–75
be ready play, 30–34
Bongs play, 43–50
Briner, R., 113

Cain, S., 98–99
campari, 58–59
career management, 4
career rewards, 4
Catch 22 situation, 84–86
Cattell, R., 21
Chunking, 45
Cialdini, R., 101–102
Clance, P. R., 22, 46
coach, 1
commitment, 69
consistency, 101
context, 70
conversational groupings, 61–63
Covey, Stephen R., 11

Dalton, S., 100
discourse play, 34–39
Don't Stay Too Late play, 64–65
Dunbar's number play, 61–66
Dweck, Carol S., 19

EAST (Easy, Attractive, Social, and
    Timely), 102–103
Economic Graph, 92–94

Eureka moments, 94–95
Eysenck, Hans J., 20, 63
Eysenckian theory, 63

face-to-face networking events, 29–30
    action immediately after the event,
        39–41
    conversation, 34–39
    preparation, 30–34
final play, 113–114
flattery, 69
Fletcher, Ben C., 21
follow-up play, 39–41
Friedman, S., 105

Gestalt therapy, 22
Googling, 32
Goyder, C., 109
Graceland (Simon), 77–79
Granovetter, Mark S., 15
Grant, A., 18
Grant, H., 67, 107

Halpern, D., 102
humblebrag, 71

Ibarra, H., 66
Imes, S. A., 22, 46 imposter play,
    17–27
imposter syndrome, 22–24
'Inner chimp', 25
Influence: The Psychology of Persuasion
    (Cialdini), 101–102

job search, 68
"Just Move on" play, 75–76

Karen J. Pine, 21
Kipling play, 83–84
Know Your Audience play, 81–96

learning, 69
likeability, 101
likeable, 107–108
LinkedIn play, 31, 82–84, 86, 90–96, 114
    profile, 87–88
    recommendations, 88–90
Little, B. R., 18, 63
Lopata, A., 46
lucky, 106

McLuhan, M., 83
Makin' Whoopee, 110–112
meat play, 89–90
mentor play, 67–79
mentors and advocates, 67, 75–76
Milgram, S., 93
Misner, I., 37

network effects, 90
networking, 5
    milestones, 24
    myths, 17–20
    nerves, 24–26
Networking Niceties, 107–108
networking niceties play, 107–108
networking playbook, 1
network smart, 105–106
"New-Age of Enlightenment," 6–9
NEXTworking play, 97–104
nudge play, 102–104

OCEAN, 41
optimal distinctiveness, 14

personal development, 5
perspective taking, 69
Peters, S., 25
plan, 11, 26
Playbook play, 1–9
power play, 84–86
process play, 29–42
professional play, 110
Putnam, R. D., 15–16

Q and A play, 73–74

Ray, G., 109
reciprocity, 101

relationships, 5, 67–68
rhyme, 57
Rule of Three, 57

scarcity, 101
Schein, E., 98
self-less play, 12–14
self-projection, 4, 5, 13, 70, 82, 88
Senge, P., 18
Simon, P., 77–79
Sinek, S., 54
small talk, 32–34, 36, 40, 51, 61, 97
SMART, 24, 30
social media, 4, 31, 48, 49, 71, 81–84, 86
social proof, 101
Social Superglue, 16
Social WD40, 16
speaking play, 108–109
staying late play, 64
Stew play, 105–106
storytelling, 56
strategic business networking, 11–16, 29, 30, 40, 51, 65–66, 84
success, 5, 19, 41, 54, 70, 78, 79
Sunstein, C., 102
"Super Sub," 58

tapping in, 43–50
Thaler, R., 102
TIARA technique, 100
Townsend, H., 56
trait theory, 21
troubleshooting play, 105–112
Twain play, 109
Twitter, 31, 32, 71, 83
2-Hour Job Search, The (Dalton), 100
type theory, 20–21

unforgiving minute, 83–84
upping our elvis, 58–59

Waldman, J., 52
Watts, D. J., 93
weak ties, 14–16
Wiseman play, 106
Wiseman, R., 106
"working a room," 17